"In *To Die Is Gain*, Dr. Roger Nutt offers his reader an impressive and theologically insightful account of the nature of the Sacrament of Anointing and its broader place in a Catholic understanding of life and death in Jesus Christ. Beginning with the universal experience of death, Nutt traces the outlines of a Christian anthropology of death within the frame of the paschal mystery, illuminating the fittingness of the signs and effects of the Sacrament of Anointing in light of this salvific reality. This book will no doubt be of great value to all who desire to deepen their appreciation for the theological and pastoral significance of the Church's sacramental encounter with the perennial realities of sin and death that mark the human experience."

FR. REGINALD LYNCH, OP
Dominican Province of St. Joseph

"This is simply the best book I've read on the Anointing of the Sick. The author is a scholar's scholar, but he writes here with clarity and practicality that both pastors and lay readers will appreciate. The anointing—which is perhaps the most neglected and misunderstood sacrament—should be an important element in any serious Catholic's spirituality. Read this book, and your gain will be incalculable."

SCOTT W. HAHN
Franciscan University of Steubenville

"This is an important book about an important, but poorly understood, sacrament. What could be more significant than serious illness and the proximity of death? What could be more important than bringing the healing grace of Christ to the seriously ill? Dr. Nutt has written a book that is theologically sound, pastorally sensitive, and spiritually rooted in the hope of Christ's Resurrection and ours. While based on the most solid scholarship it is easily accessible to the average reader. We all know someone—not to mention ourselves—who needs a deeper understanding of the great gift of the Anointing of the Sick."

RALPH MARTIN
Sacred Heart Major Seminary

To DIE Is GAIN

To DIE *Is* GAIN

A Theological (re-)Introduction *to the* Sacrament *of* Anointing of the Sick
for Clergy, Laity, Caregivers, and Everyone Else

ROGER W. NUTT

EMMAUS
ACADEMIC

Steubenville, Ohio
www.emmausacademic.com

The last enemy to be destroyed is death.
1 Corinthians 15:26

EMMAUS
A C A D E M I C

Steubenville, Ohio
www.emmausacademic.com

A Division of The St. Paul Center for Biblical Theology
Editor-in-Chief: Scott Hahn
1468 Parkview Circle
Steubenville, Ohio 43952

Library of Congress Cataloging-in-Publication Data applied for
ISBNs: 978-1-64585-196-7 hc / 978-1-64585-197-4 pb /
978-1-64585-198-1 eb

Cover design by Patty Borgman
Interior layout by Emily Demary
Cover image: Nicolas Poussin, *Extreme Unction* (1636), Fitzwilliam
Museum, Cambridge, England.

Table of Contents

Acknowledgements

My wife, Susan, and our son Timothy should be credited with coauthorship of this volume. Their support and prayers, as well as the personal sacrifices that they made during this project, sustained my work and made it possible. Words cannot express my gratitude to them.

Fr. Reginald Lynch, O.P., Matthew Levering, and Sr. Mary Diana Dreger, O.P., all gave feedback on the manuscript. I am deeply grateful for their encouragement and suggestions, which vastly improved the final product. Mrs. Grace De Salvo provided irreplaceable editorial assistance. Without her careful and thorough assistance, I would not have been able to bring this project to completion. I thank John Lawrence Nelson for his prayers and encouragement. Jennifer Nodes, Brenda Marino, Abigail Starcher, Stan Smolinski, and Mary Laurel—the entire staff of the Canizaro Library at Ave Maria University are to be thanked for their tremendous support of my work. I am grateful, too, to Scott Hahn, Chris Erickson, and the entire staff for welcoming my work to Emmaus Academic.

I taught undergraduate and graduate courses in sacramental theology for over a decade here at Ave

Maria University until an administrative appointment greatly reduced my availability to teach. I am grateful to my colleague Dr. Jeffrey Walkey for inviting me back to my old class to cover a few sessions for him. The material that we covered those days was on Anointing of the Sick. Coming back to the topic with fresh eyes and discussing the material with the great students in Dr. Walkey's class crystalized for me the importance of this material.

The whole Ave Maria University community is like family to me: students, trustees, priests, faculty, and staff. It is a privilege beyond measure to have a share in Tom Monaghan's inspiring legacy and vision for Ave Maria University, to work with so many dedicated and generous trustees, and to be a part of a university community with so many gifted and faithful colleagues and students.

My sister-in-law, Amber VanVickle, has fought cancer throughout the composition of this book. I shared a draft version of this volume with her husband, Dave. His encouragement meant more to me than he knows. Amber is a devoted wife and mother of five children ages twelve and younger: Sam, Max, Judah, Josie, and Louisa. Please keep her and their family in your prayers.

I dedicate this volume in deepest gratitude to Dr. Louis C. Argenta—a world-class scholar, a consummate friend, a trusted mentor, and an ongoing inspiration.

Introduction

St. Paul tells the Philippians that for him "to live is Christ, and to die is gain" (1:21). That attitude toward death—that it could be a gain—is foreign to most people today, even to most Christians. Human experience confirms the universality of death, and the Bible clarifies that it is a consequence of sin: "Therefore as sin came into the world through one man and death through sin, and so death spread to all men because all men sinned" (Rom 5:12). I intend for this volume to be a word of genuine theological hope in relation to a topic—death—that makes us all uncomfortable. This book is the outgrowth of an observation derived from many years of teaching sacramental theology, my own reflections on death in light of faith in Christ, and personal experiences in journeying with those in end-of-life situations. This observation is that the Sacrament of Anointing of the Sick is, perhaps, the most underappreciated gift that Christ left to his Church.

I am not claiming that Anointing of the Sick is the greatest sacrament of the Church. That would be inaccurate; the Eucharist clearly holds that place. The grace of Anointing of the Sick is not the highest spiritual reality in the life of the Church. Jesus's Body and Blood is most certainly the highest gift that the Church has received. Nor am I saying that Anointing of the Sick is the most necessary sacrament of the Church. That would also be inaccurate. Baptism is the most universally necessary sacrament of the Church. My primary claim in this book is, simply, that Anointing of the Sick is the most underappreciated gift that Christ left to his Church. The problem with the loss of an appreciation for Anointing of the Sick is that Western culture is currently in a crisis about the meaning of life, suffering, and death. We live at a time in which the doctrinal message of the sacrament of the sick and the graces that it confers are needed—more than ever. We live in a time in which the loss of an awareness of the significance of this sacrament is catastrophic. Anointing of the Sick is a proclamation and application to the dying of Christ's victory over death.

Given how vulnerable every human being is at the end of life, especially if great pain, fatigue, uncertainty, and emotional instability accompany the circumstance, the importance of a sacrament for those in danger of death is most certainly worthy of careful reflection and theological speculation. "In times of crisis," Colman O'Neill explains, "especially, when temptation is strong or when circumstances make the task of conforming to Christ more than unusually difficult, the old wounds make themselves felt again and the delicately held balance of forces becomes precarious."[1] This sacra-

---

[1] Colman E. O'Neill, *Meeting Christ in the Sacraments* (New

ment should be at the forefront of thinking about the Gospel message for those facing death, and it should be something that we desire for ourselves and our loved ones as we contemplate mortality and are confronted by death. Anointing of the Sick is thus an important aspect of the Gospel message.

It is my intention to reexplain and clarify for members of the Church today the greatness and importance of this gift so that, by being better appreciated, the gift of the sacrament can inhabit the place within the life of the Church and the life of every believer that Christ intended it to have.

The purpose of this book, therefore, is to help all Catholics—indeed, everyone—to better appreciate the profundity of this gift as a fundamental component of the Christian response to the crisis of suffering and death. It is my hope that by reflecting on the theology and spirituality contained in the Church's teaching on the sacrament of the sick that we may all rethink death, and the meaning of our lives, in light of faith in Christ's own death and resurrection. As a result, this book serves as a theological and spiritual resource for all Catholic priests and bishops, as well as seminarians, as they administer or prepare to administer this sacrament to the sick and dying. To bring Christ and the saving power of his grace to the sick and dying by conferring this sacrament is an unspeakable gift and privilege. I also write this little volume for everyone else: all believing Catholics, students and teachers of theology, health care workers, and those who are seeking to make sense out of the

---

York: Alba House, 1991), 281.

questions that stem from the reality of death and Christian claims about God.

I started writing this book before the world became shrouded in the dark cloud of the COVID-19 pandemic. Innumerable people have died from the pandemic, and everyone's lives have been impacted in significant ways. We are all thinking a little more about our own vulnerability, the fragility of life, and how superficial many of the things are that we devote our attention to on a daily basis. I am not claiming that by internalizing the theology of the Sacrament of Anointing of the Sick we will solve all our problems. However, I am now more convinced than ever that a broader and more accurate proclamation of the purpose and effects of this sacrament is utterly essential to unlocking for people the connection between the inescapable fact of death and the incessant love that God has for every human being in Christ Jesus. The place that Christ intended for this sacrament to have in the life of the Church teaches all of us a great deal about hope in the face of death, the meaning of suffering, and the ongoing presence of Christ to those who are most in need of his friendship.

The Church prepares parents for the Baptism of their children and prepares children for Confession, first Communion, and Confirmation; engaged couples go through a marriage preparation program; and candidates for the deaconate, priesthood, or religious life receive years of spiritual and intellectual formation. All of us—sooner or later—are going to die. What do we do to prepare ourselves? What formation have we received to be ready to die and to do so as an offering to God?

Christians used to prepare for death throughout their lives. They even called dying well—dying virtuously and prayerfully—an "art." Like all arts, dying well must be learned. A basic Christian conviction toward being prepared to die well is that one must live well—precisely for the sake of dying well. "The general rule," St. Robert Bellarmine explains, "'He who lives well will die well' must be mentioned before all others: for since death is nothing more than the end of life, it is certain that all who live well to the end, die well; nor can he die ill who had never lived ill. On the other hand, he who has never led a good life cannot die a good death."[2] Bellarmine, of course, does not deny the possibility of conversion for those who have not always served God throughout their lives. However, he does insist that "it is a most dangerous thing to defer until death our conversion from sin to virtue."[3] The best way to learn the "art of dying well," Bellarmine confirms, is to "attentively consider—not once, but often; not out of curiosity to learn, but out of sincere intention to live and die well—the difference between momentary things and everlasting things, between things of no importance and things of great importance."[4]

Reflecting on suffering and death in light of the sacrament of the sick, therefore, can help us to prepare ourselves under the wisdom of the Gospel for this last decisive moment of our earthly jour-

---

[2] St. Robert Bellarmine, *The Art of Dying Well (or, How to Be a Saint, Now and Forever)* (Manchester: Sophia Institute Press, 2005), 3.

[3] Bellarmine, *Dying Well*, 5.

[4] Bellarmine, *Dying Well*, 139.

ney. Knowing more about this sacrament can also ready us to be a consolation to our loved ones as they approach death. The graces of the sacrament of the sick strengthen our resolve to die well.

Nothing is more unsettling than an end-of-life situation, whether it be the result of an accident, illness, or old age. This has always been the case. However, there are more challenges today—perhaps more than ever before—that discourage people from living each day with an awareness of their mortality and the possibility of eternal life. Occasionally, a major event, like the terrorist attacks of 9/11, a natural disaster, the unexpected death of a celebrity, or a global pandemic, temporarily rouses us from our comforts and slumbers, but we usually fall back into our patterns of inattention rapidly. Neither despair nor foolhardiness is a proper Christian attitude toward death. How to prepare for the end of our earthly life or the death of a loved one in light of the Christian faith is an art that requires a level of spiritual maturity that is nearly lost today. Only pride would incline us to think that we are ready to face death on our own. Only foolishness would incline us to ignore our mortality. The spiritual maturity that is engendered by faith is a special gift or grace that comes from God and depends on him for its sustenance.

For many of us today, a pagan-like optimism toward technology, medical science, and our own moral goodness has diverted our attention away from the universality of death and the fact that death is to be embraced as the last moral action of a human life.[5] People in the West are living longer lives, which engenders an attitude of unhealthy agnosticism toward mortality. Since death seems far off and remote, we don't really ponder our mortality, vulnerability, and finitude. As the growing practice of cryonics indicates, some even think, naively, that they can put off or cheat death completely. As a result, when a serious accident or ill-

---

[5] In his 2015 encyclical letter, *Laudato Si'*, Pope Francis highlights the false sense of progress that technological advancements can inculcate: "There is a tendency to believe that every increase in power means 'an increase of "progress" itself,' an advance in 'security, usefulness, welfare and vigour; . . . an assimilation of new values into the stream of culture,' as if reality, goodness and truth automatically flow from technological and economic power as such. The fact is that 'contemporary man has not been trained to use power well,' because our immense technological development has not been accompanied by a development in human responsibility, values and conscience. Each age tends to have only a meagre awareness of its own limitations. It is possible that we do not grasp the gravity of the challenges now before us. 'The risk is growing day by day that man will not use his power as he should'; in effect, 'power is never considered in terms of the responsibility of choice which is inherent in freedom' since its 'only norms are taken from alleged necessity, from either utility or security.' But human beings are not completely autonomous. Our freedom fades when it is handed over to the blind forces of the unconscious, of immediate needs, of self-interest, and of violence. In this sense, we stand naked and exposed in the face of our ever-increasing power, lacking the wherewithal to control it. We have certain superficial mechanisms, but we cannot claim to have a sound ethics, a culture and spirituality genuinely capable of setting limits and teaching clear-minded self-restraint." Pope Francis, *Laudato Si'* (May 24, 2015), §105, https://www.vatican.va/content/francesco/en/encyclicals/documents/papa-francesco_20150524_enciclica-laudato-si.html.

ness, a pandemic, or the fragility of old age finally confronts us, we find ourselves unprepared and prone to shock or disbelief. In his short work *The Death of Ivan Ilyich*, Russian novelist Leo Tolstoy powerfully narrates the psychological horror and despair that plays out in the soul of someone ill-prepared to face their own death. Finding himself alone but unable to sleep, the dying Ivan Ilyich, Tolstoy explains,

> cried like a baby. He cried about his helplessness, about his terrible loneliness, about the cruelty of people, about the cruelty of God, about the absence of God.
>
> "Why hast Thou done all this? Why hast Thou brought me to this? What dost Thou torture me so? For what?"
>
> He did not expect an answer, and he cried because there was no answer and there could be none. The pain started up again, but he did not stir, did not call out. He said to himself, "Go on then! Hit me again! But what for? What for? What have I done to Thee?"...
>
> "What do you want?" was the first thought sufficiently intelligible to be expressed in words. "What do you want? What do you want?" he repeatedly inwardly. "What? Not to suffer. To live," he replied....
>
> His marriage—a mere accident—and his disillusionment with it, and his wife's bad breath, and the sensuality, and the pretense! And that deadly service, and those worries about money; and so it had gone for

a year, two years, ten years, twenty years—on and on in the same way. And the longer it lasted, the more deadly it became. "It's as though I had been going steadily downhill while I imagined I was going up. That's exactly what happened. In public opinion I was moving uphill, but to the same extent life was slipping away from me. And now it's gone and all I can do is die!

"What does it all mean? Why has it happened? It's inconceivable, inconceivable that life was so senseless and disgusting. And if it really was so disgusting and senseless, why should I have to die, and die in agony? Something must be wrong. Perhaps I did not live as I should have," it suddenly occurred to him. "But how could that be when I did everything one is supposed to?" he replied and immediately dismissed the one solution to the whole enigma of life and death, considering it utterly impossible. . . .

"Now comes the judgment! But I'm not guilty!" he cried out indignantly. "What is this for?" And he stopped crying and, turning his face to the wall, began to dwell on one and the same question: "Why all this horror? What is it for?"

But think as he might, he could find no answer. And when it occurred to him, as it often did, that he had not lived as he should have, he immediately recalled how correct his whole life had been and dismissed this bizarre idea.[6]

---

[6] Leo Tolstoy, *The Death of Ivan Ilyich*, trans. Lynn Solotaroff

Tolstoy's arresting account of Ivan Ilyich's deathbed despair and confusion pinpoints the mindset of many today. Medical technology has added time and quality to our lives, but it is ultimately helpless and futile in the face of death. To think otherwise, to entertain an optimism that promises some other ending besides death to our earthly lives or those of our loved ones, is to make research science and medical technology into the kind of mythical idols that drove the pagans of the ancient world into the greatest confusions and perversions. There is no more chance that medicine or technology will save us from death than there is of Zeus or Aphrodite descending from Mount Olympus to intervene on our behalf.

It is indeed true that advancements in science and medicine might be able to save us from certain causes of death for a certain time. Anyone who knows a cancer survivor, for example, is right to be grateful for these advancements. However, we should not let these fruits of modern science distract us from the fact that everyone, even those who are cured (for a time) from a particular ailment, will still come to the point when their earthly journey ends. As the despairing, regretful, doubt-filled thoughts of Tolstoy's fictional Ivan Ilyich illustrate, it should not be forgotten that, in the words of Thomas Aquinas, "fear of dangers of death has the greatest power to make man recede from the good of reason."[7]

(New York: Bantam Books, 1981), 118–20 (chapter 9).

[7] St. Thomas Aquinas, *Summa theologiae* [hereafter cited as *ST*] II-II, q. 123, a. 12: "Fortitude holds the first place, because fear of dangers of death has the greatest power to make man recede from the good of reason: and after fortitude comes

I have attempted to write this book in such a way that it does not presuppose that the reader is in possession of a complete knowledge of everything that is needed to fully appreciate and understand the role Christ intended for Anointing of the Sick to have in God's plan of salvation. The six major chapters of this book, and the twenty-five subparts of the chapters, are meant to divide the material into digestible sections that progressively build upon each other en route to a full presentation of the theology of the sacrament. The material in the early chapters and parts gives the reader an understanding of attitudes toward death today and the anthropology of sin that Anointing of the Sick aims to heal. Without understanding the nature of human life and death, sin and grace, spiritual and bodily death, and the temporal and eternal ramifications of sin, one cannot pinpoint exactly what Anointing of the Sick is supposed to accomplish in the Christian's journey toward eternal life. Starting in Chapter III, these foundational points are brought to bear on the theology of the sacrament itself. These parts help differentiate Penance and Anointing of the Sick by clarifying basic sacramental questions such as who can receive anointing, the effects of the sacrament in the order of grace, the theological significance of the rite of

---

temperance, since also pleasures of touch excel all others in hindering the good of reason." Taken from Thomas Aquinas, *Summa theologiae*, vol. 18, ed. John Mortensen and Enrique Alarcon, trans. Laurence Shapcote, O.P. (Lander, WY: The Aquinas Institute for the Study of Sacred Doctrine, 2012), 256. I am grateful to my colleague Michael Dauphinais for bringing this passage to my attention.

anointing, and the proper minister of the sacrament. The final two parts in Chapter VI, "Is Death to Be Celebrated or Mourned by Christians" and "Anointing of the Sick, Care for the Dying, and the Value of Suffering: Some (Very) Basic Bioethical Guidance," offer readers some simple principles on how the theology of Anointing of the Sick can clarify the proper Christian attitudes toward death and offer the dying sound moral guidance or assist their loved ones in making decisions on their behalf.

CHAPTER I

DEATH, LIFE, AND THE
REALITY OF SIN

Prologue: Fear of Death and How We Got Here: A Brief Review of Non-Christian Attitudes toward Death from 350 BC to AD 2540

Death has always been a foreboding mystery. Today, at least in Western societies, it has become as uncouth to speak about death as religion and politics. Even though many affirm some affiliation with the Christian religion, the Christian faith is not evident in the thought and actions of most people today, especially as regards attitudes toward death. The Western world is truly "post-Christian," and the post-Christian worldview offers no coherent understanding of death or the afterlife, so the topic of death is avoided as much as possible. In our economically comfortable and morally indifferent post-Christian societies, Joseph Ratzinger observes, "death is placed under a taboo. It is unseemly. So far as possible, it must be hidden away, the thought of it repressed in waking consciousness."[1]

As a primer to the remainder of this book, and an aid to understanding our current outlook, it is helpful to have a brief sketch of how third-millennium attitudes toward death became so divorced from the wisdom traditions of the Greco-Roman and Judeo-Christian perspectives.

The pre-Christian, Greco-Roman philosophical tradition of the West, despite not having recourse to the wisdom of the Bible and Judeo-Christian thought and culture, showed at least some measured openness to the possibility that death could have meaning, that life might continue after death, and that life after death might be an improvement over the current one. When the pagan philosopher Socrates, some 350 years before Christ, had been unjustly sentenced to death, he offered his saddened friends the following reflection:

> Let us reflect in another way, and we shall see that there is great reason to hope that death is a good, for one of two things: — either death is a state of nothingness and utter unconsciousness, or, as men say, there is a change and migration of the soul from this world to another. Now if you suppose that there is no consciousness, but a sleep like the sleep of him who is undisturbed even by the sight of dreams, death will be an unspeakable gain. . . . Now if

---

[1] Joseph Ratzinger, *Eschatology: Death and Eternal Life*, trans. Michael Waldstein (Washington, D.C.: The Catholic University of America Press, 1988), 69.

death is like this, I say that to die is gain; for eternity is then only a single night. But if death is the journey to another place, and there, as men say, all the dead are, what good, O my friends and judges, can be greater than this? If indeed when the pilgrim arrives in the world below, he is delivered from the professors of justice in this world, and finds the true judges who are said to give judgment there . . . and other sons of God who were righteous in their own life, that pilgrimage will be worth making. What would not a man give if he might converse with Orpheus and Musaeus and Hesiod and Homer? Above all, I shall be able to continue my search into true and false knowledge; as in this world, so also in that; I shall find out who is wise, and who pretends to be wise, and is not. For besides being happier in that world than in this, they will be immortal, if what is said is true.[2]

Socrates, of course, stands among the wisest and most insightful pagan philosophers in the history of philosophy. A statement such as the above seems almost unbelievable today. The last line of the same work strikes the modern reader in much the same way: "The hour of departure has arrived, and we go our ways—I to die, and you to live. Which is better God only knows."[3] Death was certainly not a

---

[2] Plato, *Apology*, trans. Benjamin Jowett, accessed on November 11, 2020, http://classics.mit.edu/Plato/apology.html.

[3] Plato, *Apology*.

taboo topic for Socrates. What he actually thought about death and the afterlife may not be so easy to discern, but he says a great deal more in the face of his own pending execution than what friends normally say among themselves today about mortality. One thing that unites a pagan like Socrates and the outlook of the Judeo-Christian tradition is that for Socrates the thought of death and the possibility of immortality or the continuation of life after death go together. In post-Christian culture, immortality has been rejected or forgotten, which causes death to stand as the absolute termination of life.

It goes without saying that not only does the reality of God provide some response to the problem of death, but God also gives meaning and purpose to life. That is to say, if there is no God, or if God is pushed to the margins, then the meaning of things in relation to God disappears. Already in the mid-1960s the Catholic Church recognized the impact that the loss of Christian doctrine and the rise of atheism would have on Western culture. In the Pastoral Constitution on the Church in the Modern World, promulgated in 1965, the Fathers of the Second Vatican Council observe: "For without the Creator the creature would disappear. . . . When God is forgotten, however, the creature itself grows unintelligible."[4] Absent God, who is the source of both being and meaning, human existence, including death, has no meaning.

The prophets of modern atheism recognized

---

[4] Second Vatican Council, *Gaudium et Spes* (December 7, 1965), §36, http://www.vatican.va/archive/hist_councils/ii_vatican_council/documents/vat-ii_const_19651207_gaudium-et-spes_en.html.

and accepted the logical consequences of the denial of God in relation to death more so than their causal adherents and novice confessors. The dogmatic atheists exalted absolute freedom—unhinged power—over every other value. Meaning and purpose appear to restrain freedom. The rejection of God frees humanity from the need to follow his purpose and seek his will. Only death remains as the last, immovable check on absolute freedom. For Friedrich Nietzsche (+1900), the animal-like human being, the human being freed from the shackles of faith and moral tradition, becomes "overman" (superman), who makes meaning for himself. Rather than seeing himself as subordinate to God and called to follow God's plan, the overman is over everything and subject to nothing:

> Behold, I teach you the overman. The overman is the meaning of the earth. Let your will say: the overman shall be the meaning of the earth! I beseech you, my brothers, remain faithful to the earth, and do not believe those who speak to you of otherworldly hopes! Poison-mixers are they, decaying and poisoned themselves, of whom the earth is weary: so let them go.
>
> Once the sin against God was the greatest sin; but God died, and these sinners died with him. To sin against the earth is now the most dreadful thing, and to esteem the entrails of the unknowable higher than the meaning of the earth.[5]

---

[5]   Friedrich Nietzsche, *Thus Spoke Zarathustra*, §3, in *The Porta-*

Because God has died, according to Nietzsche, there is no sin—no sinners—only the will of the superhumans, who, now that they are free from God and the Judeo-Christian moral system, place themselves over everything—beyond good and evil. Each person, then, becomes a god unto himself. Nietzsche understood the implications of this radical human-centered atheism: "Human existence is uncanny and still without meaning," he admits.[6]

Many variations and modifications of Nietzsche's thought emerged in the twentieth century. The problem of death, the ultimate trump card against radical freedom, became a near omnipresent concern of the existentialists. The French existentialist philosopher Jean-Paul Sartre explains the purposelessness of life and death in terms of mere facticity. Birth and death have no meaning; they are simple facts. "Death is never that which gives meaning to life," Sartre argues. "It is, on the contrary, that which deprives life of all significance. If we have to die, our life has no sense because our problems do not receive any kind of solution and because the very meaning of the problems remains undetermined."[7] So even if human beings live out their freedom without restraint, creating themselves as they see fit without reference to an overarching plan or purpose, they still suffer the inescapable fate of death.

---

ble Nietzsche, trans. Walter Kaufmann (New York: The Viking Press, 1964), 125.

[6] Nietzsche, *Thus Spoke Zarathustra*, §3 (p. 132).

[7] Jean-Paul Sartre, *L'être and le néant* [*Being and Nothingness*] (Paris: Gallimard, 1955), 624, cited in Jacques Choron, *Death and Western Thought* (New York: Macmillan, 1963), 244.

Sartre's contemporary, the French writer Albert Camus, develops the implications of atheistic purposelessness throughout his writings and especially in his essay "The Myth of Sisyphus." Sisyphus is the tragic figure from Greek mythology who is condemned by the gods to futility by spending eternity rolling a rock uphill only to have it roll down again before he can deposit it at the top. Camus's provocation in this essay is that if life and death have no meaning, suicide—using freedom to control even death—becomes the ultimate question for humanity. Why let death cancel our absolute claims to freedom? Given that life and death have no meaning, according to Camus, why not control them with our freedom by taking our lives into our own hands? How one ends one's life acts as a kind of confession about what he thinks of the meaning of life. "Killing yourself amounts to confessing," Camus argues:

> It is confessing that life is too much for you or that you do not understand it. Let's not go too far in such analogies, however, but rather return to everyday words. It is merely confessing that that "is not worth the trouble." Living, naturally, is never easy. You continue making the gestures commanded by existence for many reasons, the first of which is habit. Dying voluntarily implies that you have recognized, even instinctively, the ridiculous character of that habit, the absence of any profound reason for living, the insane character of

that daily agitation, and the uselessness of suffering.[8]

Camus's argument, for all of its faults, does press the position to its logical consequences. How one views the meaning of life is related to what one thinks about the meaning of death and what comes after, if anything. And, conversely, how one dies (or chooses to die) says what one thinks about the meaning of life and what might come after this life. If life is merely pointless, like the futility of Sisyphus, the endless and hopeless rock-pushing curse, then what purpose is there in living?

While many people in the postmodern world do not order their lives according to a divinely ordained purpose or plan, they are not quite willing to confront death in as provocative a fashion as the atheistic philosophers. As a result, people need distractions to prevent them from pondering the hopelessness of this perspective. In his famed futuristic dystopian novel, *Brave New World*, set in the year 2540, Aldous Huxley describes how hospitals in the godless "new world" are set up to distract people from death and void it of any personal significance. Huxley's fictitious culture sounds very much like the post-Christian world that we now live in. One of the main characters, Linda, ends up in a hospital structured according to the ideas of the new world:

> Linda was dying in company—in company with all modern conveniences. The air was

---

8   Albert Camus, *The Myth of Sisyphus and Other Essays*, trans. Justin O'Brien (New York: Vintage Books, 1991), 5–6.

continuously alive with gay synthetic melodies. At the foot of every bed, confronting its moribund occupant, was a television box. Television was left on, a running tap, from morning till night. Every quarter of an hour, the prevailing perfume of the room was automatically changed.[9]

Linda passes away suddenly in this hospital in the presence of her son, John. John is grief-stricken at his mother's passing and seeks a nurse. The nurse, however, is not concerned about the deceased patient but about John's uncouth reaction to his mother's death. She wonders how to handle the situation:

> Should she speak to him? try to bring him back to a sense of decency? remind him of where he was? of what fatal mischief he might do to these poor innocents? Undoing all their wholesome death-conditioning with this disgusting outcry—as though death were something terrible, as though any one mattered as much as all that! It might give them the most disastrous ideas about the subject, might upset them into reacting in the entirely wrong, the utterly anti-social way.[10]

---

[9] Aldous Huxley, *Brave New World* (New York: Harper and Row, 1989), 203. Cited by Matthew Levering, introduction to *On Christian Dying*, ed. Matthew Levering (Lanham: Rowman and Littlefield Publishers, Inc., 2004), xii.

[10] Huxley, *Brave New World*, 211–12, in Levering, *On Christian Dying*, xiii.

So Huxley's new world of the future seeks to distract people from death, from ever thinking or reflecting on the possibility that their lives might actually matter. The dystopian world conditions people to avoid thinking about life's meaning and to live and die as if nothing and no one had a purpose beyond this world. The vision advocated by Huxley mixes the godless-meaningless view of the existentialists and the materialistic worldview that also colors people's thinking today.

A certain superficial view of scientific progress has promised to solve all of humanity's problems. Its failure to do this led, in part, to the disenchantment manifest in the existentialist and postmodernist authors of the twentieth century, like Camus. Since nature has not been brought into a controllable order, especially the realities of suffering and death, scientific knowledge became a means of producing death under technological control. Abortion, euthanasia, assisted suicide, and other technologically induced forms of death are expressions of this materialistic, purposeless mindset. That unwanted lives can be aborted and the lives of the sick and aged can be terminated, in both cases with great technological precision, is a product of a culture that cannot see meaning in life, suffering, and death and cannot live without ultimate control. "By becoming a product," Joseph Ratzinger observes,

> death is supposed to vanish as a question mark about the nature of being human, a more-than-technological enquiry. The issue of euthanasia is becoming increas-

ingly important because people wish to avoid death as something which happens *to me*, and replace it with a technical cessation of function which I do not need to carry out myself.[11]

This leaves humanity with nowhere to turn. Atheism insisting on meaningless and modern science has not saved us from death, although it has become adept at bringing it about. In either scenario, death is unbearable. Confirming this point, Cardinal Robert Sarah notes:

> Nowadays Western societies reject death, traumatized by the pain and grieving that accompany it. Modern man would like to be immortal. This denial of the great passage leads to a culture of death that permeates social relations as a whole. Postmodern civilization denies death, causes it, and paradoxically unceasingly exalts it. The assassination of God allows death to keep prowling all the time, because hope no longer dwells within the horizon of men.[12]

The rejection of God and the loss of meaning go hand in hand. It is understandable why philosophers and authors who reject God also reject the idea that life, death, and suffering have any meaning or purpose beyond the freedom of expression

---

[11] Ratzinger, *Eschatology*, 71.

[12] Robert Cardinal Sarah, *The Power of Silence: Against the Dictatorship of Noise*, trans. Michael Miller (San Francisco: Ignatius Press, 2017), 182 (no. 351).

with which each human informs their own existence. Medical doctor L. S. Dugdale pinpoints a
shift that took place between the Christian "art
of dying" attitude toward life and death and the
postmodern flight from death: "Whereas the *ars
moriendi* taught that a person cultivated good life
habits with a view to dying well, the early twentieth century came to focus solely on living well—
death and dying be damned."[13]

The contention of this book is that life does have
meaning and that death and suffering can be accepted
in a way that makes them moral and meritorious elements in God's redemptive plan.[14] Death and suffering have to be accepted and offered to God with love,
patience, and courage. God did not inflict the miseries of this world upon humanity, but he does redeem
us from them in Christ. Anointing of the Sick gives
the suffering and dying special graces to die in union
with God, to die with purpose according to God's
redemptive plan, to die so as to enter eternal glory—
to die in the most fulfilling way possible.

It is beyond the scope of this book to engage
in a point-by-point refutation of these modern,
atheistic views of life and death. The point of the
inclusion of the material in this chapter is simply
to help the reader (pastor, teacher, or student) to
understand current attitudes toward death. To proclaim the Gospel in an efficacious and penetrating

---

[13] L. S. Dugdale, *The Lost Art of Dying: Reviving Forgotten
Wisdom* (New York: Harper Collins Publishers, 2020), 42–43.

[14] For a defense of a Christian approach to death in the context
of modern political theory and postmodernism, see Marc D.
Guerra, "The Use and Abuse of Thanatos in Life," *Perspectives
on Political Science* 37, no. 3 (2008): 136–41.

manner, Christians must understand the mindset of their contemporaries. The purposelessness of life and the inescapability of death haunt human beings who live in the comforts of the first world. Like the conditioned members of Huxley's futuristic "World State," many today try at all costs to avoid thinking of death, many never think of living so as to die well, and many are ignorant of the truth that death has been redeemed and therefore is not a meaningless end to a pointless existence.

Even if believing Christians today do not adhere to the ultimate conclusions of thinkers like Nietzsche, Sartre, Camus, and Huxley, even if they do not wish to live in the brave new world where everything aims to distract people from death, the ideas that these authors champion still exercise influence over our view of the world. As Ratzinger noted above, it is no accident that contemporary Western cultures attempt to keep death out of sight. It is important for all of us to examine our attitude toward death, to try to discern its genealogy. It is important for pastors, health care workers, and everyone who might care for or be in the presence of someone who is dying to understand the consequential ideas about death that have crept into the very marrow of the culture that we live in.

Life, Death, and Christian Anthropology: A Short Introduction

Now that we have briefly examined some of the steps that have led us down the path to our current attitudes toward death, some presentation of the true nature of life and death is necessary. As a transition to a Christian understanding of life and death, a brief reference to another twentieth-century writer is illustrative. After being an agnostic for most of his life, Malcolm Muggeridge converted to Christianity and then to Catholicism. In the late 1960s, Muggeridge was largely responsible for making known to the Western, English-speaking world the amazing work of charity that Mother Teresa and her sisters were doing for the poor and dying in Calcutta, India. His conversion to Catholicism was due in part to the impact of meeting Mother Teresa and seeing her work in the slums of Calcutta. Muggeridge produced a documentary film on Mother Teresa's work and wrote a famous book on the same topic, *Something Beautiful for God*. Mother's attitude toward the reality of death had a deep impact on Muggeridge's internalization of the Christian faith. Her response runs completely counter to the attitude toward death advocated by the authors examined above. Mother Teresa told Muggeridge of her work to care for a destitute woman who was dying in the street: "The first woman I saw I myself picked her up from the street. She had been half eaten by the rats and ants. I took her to the hospital but they could not do anything for her."[15] Muggeridge asks Mother Teresa why she tries to care for people like this woman for whom nothing could be done—why care for people who are so hopelessly ill that they are bound to die anyway? Her response to his question is striking:

---

[15] Cited by Levering in the introduction to *On Christian Dying*, x.

> First of all we want to make them feel that they are wanted, we want them to know that there are people who really love them, who really want them, at least for the few hours that they have to live, to know human and divine love. That they too may know that they are the children of God, and that they are not forgotten and that they are loved and cared about and there are young lives ready to give themselves in their service.[16]

Mother Teresa's service to the poorest of the poor, especially the dying, was not to seek to save them from death or to ignore their mortality. She did not try to distract them or console them with hollow platitudes (e.g., "everything is going to be all right"). She served the dying to help them die well—to die loved and in the knowledge that they are children of God. Unlike the atheistic authors cited in the prologue or the modern tendency to use technology to "produce" death to avoid suffering, Mother Teresa faced death and ministered to the dying because she understood that life and death are not meaningless. For Mother Teresa, it was not dying that was the ultimate tragedy but dying without knowing that one is loved, especially by God. Her charity toward the dying unveils deep channels of wisdom and insight from within the patrimony of the Christian faith. Priests, family

---

[16] Malcolm Muggeridge, *Something Beautiful for God: Mother Teresa of Calcutta* (San Francisco: Harper and Row, 1971), 91–92. Cited by Matthew Levering, introduction to *On Christian Dying*, x–xi.

members, friends, and health care workers need to be able to love and minister to the dying with this same courage and fidelity to the Gospel message.

Life: A Brief Sketch

Death is one of the "last things" treated in the branch of theology known as "eschatology." Coming prior to judgment, purgatory, hell, or heaven, death is the first of the very last things in the journey of human life from earth to eternity. Death and life are understood in light of each other. Given that death is a privation of life on earth, some understanding of life is necessary to forge a proper comprehension of these realities.

The first and most important truth about life is that it is what theologians and philosophers call an "analogical reality." This means that life is found and possessed in various degrees by beings of diverse orders of perfection. The perfection of the reality of life itself is found in God. Any other created form of life, whether it be angelic, human, animal, or vegetative, is a finite participation in God's own fullness of life. The Bible speaks clearly and repeatedly of God as living: "My heart and flesh sing for joy to the living God" (Ps 84:2). God's life is not determined by any finite power or potential but is infinite and infinitely perfect. In fact, the personal name for himself that God discloses to Moses in Exodus 3:14 indicates the fullness of life that he possesses: "I AM WHO I AM." Thomas Aquinas explains that the word "life" is not only truly said of God but that the reality of life is most fully realized in God: "That being whose act of understanding is its very nature, and which, in what it naturally possesses, is not determined by another, must have life in the most perfect degree. Such is God; and hence in him principally is life."[17]

What it means to be alive as a creature, then, is that there is something within living beings that enlivens them, something that gives them a finite and created participation in the infinitely full life of God. "All things are said to be alive," Aquinas explains, "that determine themselves to movement or operation of any kind."[18] The self-determination or movement that Aquinas associates with being alive in this passage is not an external activity like running or jumping or manual labor. To be alive is not an external property of something, but a way of existing that has some internal source of vitality within the living thing itself. The Christian theologians of the Middle Ages loved to quote a passage from *De anima*, the Greek philosopher Aristotle's work on the soul, to explain this point: "In living things, to live is to be" (*vivere viventibus est esse*).[19] Plant growth, for example, is something

---

[17] Thomas Aquinas, *ST* I, q. 18, a. 3. Taken from Thomas Aquinas, *Summa theologiae*, vol. 13, ed. John Mortensen and Enrique Alarcon, trans. Laurence Shapcote, O.P. (Lander, WY: The Aquinas Institute for the Study of Sacred Doctrine, 2012), 204.

[18] Thomas Aquinas, *ST* I, q. 18, a. 1 (p. 204).

[19] Aristotle, *De anima*, II.4 (415a23–415b28), which can be found with St. Thomas Aquinas's commentary in *Aristotle's De Anima in the Version of William Moerbeke and the Commentary of St. Thomas Aquinas*, trans. Kenelm Foster and Silvester Humphries (New Haven, CT: Yale University Press, 1951), 211.

that comes from within the life of the plant, even though plant life is nourished by water and sunlight. Animals move around and sense things because the principles of animal movement are within them. Human beings can grow, move, sense, and also know, understand, and love because all of these powers are within each existing human nature. When a human being understands something, the activity is not an external action but is instead an active power at work within the one understanding. Conversely, rocks can be heated or cooled, thrown or dropped, but they are not said to be alive, because the "movement" of being heated or dropped does not unfold by any interior principle within the existence of rock. The form of heat or physical movement is applied to the rock by some external agent.

The uniqueness of human life in relation to God is indicated in the Bible when, as his last creative act on the sixth day of creation, God says (Gen 1:26): "Let us make man in our image, after our likeness." Genesis 2 clarifies the uniqueness of human life by adding that it is by the very breath of God, and not merely being bodily matter, that humanity is made alive (Gen 2:7): "then the LORD God formed man of dust from the ground, and breathed into his nostrils the breath of life; and man became a living soul." This means that human life, while being bodily, is not reducible to material existence. The ancient Greek language used two words for life, *bios* and *zoe*. The Greek word for "breath of life" used in Genesis 2 is *zoe*. This point is significant for understanding the uniqueness of human life. "Unlike *bios*," Scott Hahn explains, "*zoe* conveys so much more than mere physical existence.

God didn't just breathe air into Adam's nostrils; he breathed *life*—spiritual life, eternal life, divine life. He breathed his own life into Adam."[20]

The spiritual principle within human beings—the soul—gives human life a unique meaning—namely, that it is made for a relationship with God, and not merely for the enjoyment of created things and earthly existence. Being a person transcends the confines of the temporal and material order.[21] Human beings (and angels) can "live" in communion with God by living according to the unique principle of life that God gave us. "In Sacred Scripture the term 'soul,'" the *Catechism the of the Catholic Church* explains, "often refers to human *life* or the entire human *person*. But 'soul' also refers to the innermost aspect of man, that which is of greatest value in him, that by which he is most especially in God's image: 'soul' signifies the *spiritual principle* in man."[22] The reality of human life as uniquely biological, intellectual, spiritual, and capable of special union with God through grace is something deeply underscored in the Gospel of John. The Fourth Gospel carefully shows how Christ's redemptive work is ordered to healing and elevating fallen human life through Christ's fullness. It is striking to read St. John's repeated use of the word "life" (emphasis added):

---

[20] Scott Hahn, *Hope to Die: The Christian Meaning of Death and the Resurrection of the Body* (Steubenville, OH: Emmaus Road Publishing, 2020), 11.

[21] On this point, see Carlo Leget, *Living with God: Thomas Aquinas on the Relation between Life on Earth and "Life" after Death* (Leuven: Peeters, 1997), 262–65.

[22] *Catechism of the Catholic Church,* 2nd ed. (New York: Doubleday, 1995), 363.

1:4: "In him was *life*, and the *life* was the light of men."

3:16: "For God so loved the world that he gave his only-begotten Son, that whoever believes in him should not perish but have *eternal life*."

3:36: "He who believes in the Son has *eternal life*; he who does not obey the Son shall not see *life*, but the wrath of God rests upon him."

5:21: "For as the Father raises the dead and gives them *life*, so also the Son gives *life* to whom he will."

5:26: "For the Father has *life* in himself, so he has granted the Son also to have *life* in himself."

6:35: "Jesus said to them, 'I am the bread of *life*; he who comes to me shall not hunger, and he who believes in me shall never thirst.'"

6:53: "Jesus said to them, 'Truly, truly, I say to you, unless you eat the flesh of the Son of man and drink his blood, you have no *life* in you; he who eats my flesh and drinks my blood has *eternal life*, and I will raise him up at the last day."

6:58: "This is the bread which came down from heaven, not such as the fathers ate and died; he who eats this bread will *live for ever*."

11:25: "I am the resurrection and the *life*; he who believes in me, though he die, yet shall he *live*."

12:24–25: "Truly, truly, I say to you, unless

a grain of wheat fall into the earth and dies, it remains alone; but if it dies, it bears much fruit. He who loves his *life* loses it, and he who hates his *life* in this world will keep it for *eternal life*."

14:6: "I am the way, and the truth, and the *life*."

17:3: "This is *eternal life*, that they know you the only true God, and Jesus Christ whom you have sent."

Being alive, therefore, is not reducible to what one does for a living (e.g., "army life") or the type of external activity, like jogging, that human beings engage in. Human life is a unique way of existing that participates, by both nature and grace, in the fullness of life possessed by God himself. The gift of grace merited by Christ's work gives human beings a special elevated share in God's own life—a participation—as St. Peter explains in his second letter (1:4): "he has granted to us his precious and very great promises, that through these you may escape from the corruption that is in the world because of passion, and become partakers of the divine nature." This unique participation in life that human beings enjoy is the result of Christ's conquest over death and the restoration of the divine image that was lost through sin.

God's life is perfect and eternal. Through Christ and the outpouring of the Holy Spirit, human life is healed and elevated. This is why the Fathers of the First Council of Nicaea (AD 325) and the First Council of Constantinople (AD 381) referred to the Holy Spirit as the "Lord, the giver of life" in the Creed. "In our own age, then," John Paul II teaches, "we are called anew by the ever ancient and ever new faith of the Church, to draw near to the Holy Spirit as the giver of life."[23]

Death and Eternal Life: An Outline

Because human life is lived as a union of body and soul, death is not an extinction or annihilation of life. When the sensate life of an animal ceases, its "life"—principle of living—ends. When the nutritive life of a plant ceases, its life ends. When the internal principle of life ceases to animate a living thing, when the source of its life is extinguished, it is said to die. However, because human *life* is not reducible to the physical movements of growth and sensation but is informed and animated by the life of a rational soul, the biological death of the human body is not the end of human life. Thus, even though death deprives living things of life in some sense, for human beings death entails the separation of the body and soul but not the extinction of the soul.[24]

The truth that death is not an annihilation of human life is progressively revealed in the Old

---

[23] St. John Paul II, *Dominum et Vivificantem*: *On the Holy Spirit in the Life of the Church and the World* (May 18, 1986), §2.1, http://www.vatican.va/content/john-paul-ii/en/encyclicals/documents/hf_jp-ii_enc_18051986_dominum-et-vivificantem.html.

[24] For a discussion of Aquinas's view of death as privation and death as separation of soul and body, see Leget, *Living with God*, 68–95.

Testament. In the Book of Daniel (12:2), to provide just one example, the prophet teaches: "And many of those who sleep in the dust of the earth shall awake, some to everlasting life, and some to shame and everlasting contempt."

Ultimately, following upon the redemptive power of Christ's own bodily resurrection and ascension into heaven, the Christian faith teaches that the bodies and souls of the faithful departed will be reunited and that the risen person will enjoy eternal beatitude as a body-soul composite. "In death, the separation of the soul from the body," the *Catechism* teaches, "the human body decays and the soul goes to meet God, while awaiting its reunion with its glorified body. God, in his almighty power, will definitively grant incorruptible life to our bodies by reuniting them with our souls, through the power of Jesus' Resurrection."[25] This truth of the separation of soul from body at death and their final restoration at the final judgment is revealed by Christ's own life and the bodily assumption of the Virgin Mary, and it is affirmed in many places in Scripture.

For example, in one of the heavenly visions that St. John is given in the Book of Revelation (6:9–10), he sees the "souls" of Christian martyrs under the heavenly altar praying for justice: "I saw under the altar the souls of those who had been slain for the word of God and for the witness they had borne; they cried out with a loud voice, 'O Sovereign Lord, holy and true, how long before you will judge and avenge our blood on those who

---

[25] *CCC*, 997.

dwell upon the earth?'" At the final judgment, when Christ descends from heaven, Paul teaches (1 Thess 4:16, 17) that "the dead in Christ will rise first . . . and so we shall always be with the Lord."

Christian doctrine clarifies the resurrection of the body is not merely a return to biological life. Ongoing or everlasting earthly life is not the object of Christian hope. Life in the resurrection, while it is truly bodily, is a new state of existence in which all of the consequences of sin and the Fall are transformed by Christ's victory over death. In one of the final visions of the Book of Revelation (21:2–4; emphasis added), St. John describes the unveiling of a new heaven and a new earth:

> I saw the holy city, new Jerusalem, coming down out of heaven from God, prepared as a bride adorned for her husband; and I heard a great voice from the throne saying, "Behold, the dwelling of God is with men. He will dwell with them, and they shall be his people, and God himself will be with them; he will wipe away every tear from their eyes, and *death shall be no more*, neither shall there be mourning nor crying nor pain any more, for the former things have passed away."

Human life, therefore, because of its unique creation in the divine image as a body-soul composite with a rational soul capable of eternal union with God, is not confined to the biological timetable that it passes on earth, nor is it fulfilled by earthly realities. In fact, when the Church offers a Mass for the dead, in one of the prefaces to the Eucharistic prayer she affirms that the life of the deceased is not erased: "Lord, for your faithful people life is changed, not ended. When the body of our earthly dwelling lies in death we gain an everlasting dwelling place in heaven."[26]

Because death is not the extinction of human existence, earthly life is often described by the Christian tradition as a "way" or "pilgrim journey." Earth and this life are not meant to be the permanent or lasting dwelling of human beings. In the Dogmatic Constitution on the Church, *Lumen Gentium*, the Fathers of Vatican II remind the faithful that this life with all of its imperfections is not the lasting home and final destiny of human beings. Earthly life is a pilgrim journey toward our heavenly homeland:

> All the members ought to be molded in the likeness of Him, until Christ be formed in them. For this reason we, who have been made to conform with Him, who have died with Him and risen with Him, are taken up into the mysteries of His life, until we will reign together with Him. On earth, still as pilgrims in a strange land, tracing in trial and in oppression the paths He trod, we are made one with His sufferings like the body is one with the Head, suffering with Him, that with Him we may be glorified.[27]

---

[26] *Roman Missal*, Preface of Christian Death I. Cited in *CCC*, 1012.

[27] Second Vatican Council, *Lumen Gentium* (November 21, 1964), §7, http://www.vatican.va/archive/hist_councils/

Eastern Orthodox theologian Alexander Schmemann explains that death itself was changed by Christ: "It is our whole faith that by His own death Christ changed the very nature of death, made it a passage—a 'passover,' a 'Pascha'—into the Kingdom of God."[28] This outlook is something with which most Christians today have lost touch. The Anointing of the Sick is a gift from Christ to help us pass from this life to eternal glory, and a retrieval of the theology of this sacrament can serve as an evangelical and catechetical tool to assist followers of Christ in shaping a faith-informed view of death and dying as a passage from this life to the next.

More will be added in this and subsequent chapters to integrate how life, suffering, and death are related to the Sacrament of Anointing of the Sick. However, the purpose of the material in this first chapter is simply to give the reader some basic tools that are needed to appreciate the issues that are related to the sacrament of the sick. Indeed, the effect of sin and its remnants are important aspects of human experience that require further clarification in relation to the specific theology of this sacrament. Nevertheless, one preliminary conclusion that should be accentuated is that the biblical doctrine of healing, which is realized most fully in bodily resurrection and eternal life,

---

ii_vatican_council/documents/vat-ii_const_19641121_lumen-gentium_en.html.

[28] Alexander Schmemann, *Great Lent: Journey to Pascha*, rev. ed. (Crestwood, N.Y.: St. Vladimir's Seminary Press, 1974), 12. Cited by Matthew Levering in *Jesus and the Demise of Death: Resurrection, Afterlife, and the Fate of the Christian* (Waco TX: Baylor University Press, 2012), 2.

ought not to be conflated with a scientific-medicinal understanding of cure.[29] Following the work of Fr. Christopher Saliga, Fr. Paul Jerome Keller points out that we must distinguish between "healing" in the theological sense of being saved by God and "cure" in a medical sense. Presenting Saliga's insights, Keller explains:

> He writes about the misunderstanding regarding the anointing of the sick when it is thought to be the only alternative left, a sacramental last-ditch effort or placebo-type palliative intervention. A cure, he says, "refers to a patient's scientifically measurable positive response to a therapeutic intervention or a combination of such interventions." Someone with a severe infection may be said to be cured when medical treatment has been successful. "Healing" within the Catholic sphere, however, is something that transcends temporality: It "may or may not involve cure even when cure is fairly holistically defined. This is the case because healing is understood relative to the ultimate reason for which we exist, the face-to-face beatific union with God for all eternity."[30]

---

[29] I am indebted to the work of John C. Kasza for the distinction between full eschatological healing and medicinal healing. See John C. Kasza, *Understanding Sacramental Healing: Anointing and Viaticum* (Chicago: Hillenbrand Books, 2007), esp. 21.

[30] Paul Jerome Keller, O.P., *101 Questions & Answers on the Sacraments of Healing: Penance and Anointing of the Sick* (New York/Mahwah: Paulist Press, 2010), 106–7.

This is why the Church, in her prayer for the dying or recently deceased, commends them to God in the next life. The Church does not view death as the cessation of life as such. The *Catechism* explains the connection between the end of this life in death and entrance into eternal life in this way:

> The Christian who unites his own death to that of Jesus views it as a step towards him and an entrance into everlasting life. When the Church for the last time speaks Christ's words of pardon and absolution over the dying Christian, seals him for the last time with a strengthening anointing, and gives him Christ in viaticum as nourishment for the journey, she speaks with gentle assurance:
>
> Go forth, Christian soul, from this world
> in the name of God the almighty Father,
> who created you,
> in the name of Jesus Christ, the Son of the living God,
> who suffered for you,
> in the name of the Holy Spirit,
> who was poured out upon you.
> Go forth, faithful Christian!
>
> May you live in peace this day,
> may your home be with God in Zion,
> with Mary, the virgin Mother of God,
> with Joseph, and all the angels and saints.
> . . .

> May you return to [your Creator]
> who formed you from the dust of the earth.
> May holy Mary, the angels, and all the saints
> come to meet you as you go forth from this life. . . .
>
> May you see your Redeemer face to face.[31]

In the modern world, healing is almost completely associated with the cure of an ailment. In this view, healing works like medicine: you take the pill, and the headache goes away; you pray for healing, and the sickness is cured. However, while miraculous healing is real and has a place in God's plan, this view of healing is extremely narrow and uninformed by the significance of Christ's death and resurrection. It is also not the primary effect of Anointing of the Sick or the proper object of Christian hope. As Keller explains, again quoting the work of Saliga, "The question for you and me is both simple and frightening: 'Do I trust God enough to pray in union with Jesus in the Garden?' If I do, I am well disposed to receive God's healing (sanctifying) graces via specific sacramental interventions, such as anointing of the sick, graces that may or may not cause curative effects in 'this' situation."[32] The healing that Christ merited for humanity is not like modern medicine. Modern medicine cures many significant ailments, but God's healing brings salvation and eternal life.

---

[31] *CCC*, 1020.

[32] Keller, O.P., *The Sacraments of Healing*, 107.

As human beings age and struggle with illness, St. John Paul II counsels them to embrace the time they have and make it spiritually productive in light of the Christian message:

> In Christ, death—tragic and disconcerting as it is—is redeemed and transformed; it is even revealed as a "sister" who leads us to the arms of our Father.
>
> Faith thus illuminates the mystery of death and brings serenity to old age, now no longer considered and lived passively as the expectation of a calamity but rather as a promise-filled approach to the goal of full maturity. These are years to be lived with a sense of trusting abandonment into the hands of God, our provident and merciful Father. It is a time to be used creatively for deepening our spiritual life through more fervent prayer and commitment to the service of our brothers and sisters in charity.[33]

Such wisdom, rooted in the Christian faith, is drastically in need of recovery today.[34] Unpacking the theology of Anointing of the Sick pinpoints just how suffering due to illness or old age can indeed

---

[33] St. John Paul II, *Letter of His Holiness Pope John Paul II to the Elderly* (1999), §15.2–16.1, http://www.vatican.va/content/john-paul-ii/en/letters/1999/documents/hf_jp-ii_let_01101999_elderly.html.

[34] For a profound theological response to the problem of death and suffering in light of the Christian teaching on the virtues, see Matthew Levering, *Dying and the Virtues* (Grand Rapids, MI: William B. Eerdmans Publishing Company, 2018). This work includes a chapter on the virtue of surrender and Anointing of the Sick.

be embraced as a meaningful and fruitful opportunity within God's plan of salvation.

Chapter II

Theological Foundations of the Sacrament of the Sick

Biblical Foundations of the Sacrament of Anointing of the Sick

Evagrius Ponticus (b. 345) was one of the most influential spiritual writers of the early Church. Evagrius wrote a short work titled in Greek *The Praktikos*, which can be loosely translated as "practices."[1] Running counter to our modern notion of "practice" or "praxis," which reduces things to external action, Evagrius sees the "practices" of the faith as not primarily external works or activities. The first "chapter" or axiom of his *Praktikos* states that "Christianity is the dogma of Christ our Savior. It is composed of *praktike*, of the contemplation of the physical world and of the con-

---

[1] Evagrius Ponticus, *The Praktikos and Chapters on Prayer*, trans. John Eudes Bamberger (Kalamazoo, MI: Cistercian Publications, 1981).

templation of God."[2] It is strange for our modern ears to hear the "practice" of the faith spoken of in such impractical terms like "dogma" and "contemplation." There is, however, an important lesson in this short statement for Christians today. The practice of the Christian faith is not something that is simply "done," like working out or watching a movie. The practice of the faith is something that is lived—an all-encompassing way of life. As Joseph Ratzinger explains:

> Christian faith favors life. It believes in that God who is the God of the living. Its goal is life, and so it assents to life on all its levels as a gift and reflection of the God who is life itself. It assents to life even in its overshadowing by suffering. For even then life remains a gift of God, opening up for us new possibilities of existence and meaning. For Christian faith there is no such thing as a life not worth living. Life, with all its shadow side, remains the gift of God, entrusted to us as companions who by loving service one of another acquire true riches and liberty.[3]

This way of life comes from living in communion with God through the gracious gifts of faith, hope, and charity by contemplating Christ's own life and teachings (dogmas). For St. Paul, the dogma of

---

[2] Ponticus, *The Praktikos*, 15.

[3] Joseph Ratzinger, *Eschatology: Death and Eternal Life*, trans. Michael Waldstein (Washington, D.C.: The Catholic University of America Press, 1988), 101.

Christ's death and resurrection was a consolation and guiding light for how to live, suffer, and die as a follower of Jesus. In 2 Timothy (2:11–13), Paul offers Timothy the following saying: "If we have died with him, we shall also live with him; if we endure, we shall also reign with him; if we deny him, he also will deny us; if we are faithless, he remains faithful—for he cannot deny himself."

An important part of Christ's life and teaching is his own ministry to the sick and suffering, as well as the directions that he gave to his Apostles regarding the care of the sick. And, of course, Christ's own suffering, death, and resurrection reveal how Christians ought to approach their own mortality and understand life after death.

In the famous hymn of Philippians 2, St. Paul teaches that Christ's death was not merely something that (passively) happened to him but was more properly an act of obedience to the Father: "he humbled himself *and become obedient unto death*, even death on a cross" (2:8; emphasis added). Paul also notes that because Jesus was obedient unto death, "God has highly exalted him and bestowed on him the name which is above every name" (Phil 2:9).[4] The "dogma of Christ our Savior" that Evagrius sets forth to be "practiced" by contemplation,

---

[4] For a presentation of how Paul's teaching on Christ's obedience unto death was adopted by Thomas Aquinas in key areas of his understanding of martyrdom and Christ's death on the Cross, see Roger Nutt, "'Obedient unto Death': The Function of Philippians 2 in St. Thomas's Theology of the Cross" in *Thomas Aquinas, Biblical Theologian*, ed. Michael Dauphinais and Roger Nutt (Steubenville, OH: Emmaus Academic, 2021), 231–47.

therefore, includes an important message about death and suffering, as well as Christ's attitude toward death and how his followers ought to view death in light of his life and teachings.

Indeed, we might say that the Gospel message teaches us how to live with our mortality and how to live so that we might die for God and in union with him, in the hope that like Christ we too might be exalted by the Father. Understanding Anointing of the Sick as a Christian "practice" of the dogma of Christ is, therefore, pivotal in how a Christian practices the life of faith as a journey toward eternal life.

There is another layer to the Christian anthropology that was sketched above, especially regarding the effects of the Fall and sin, original and personal, on the human condition in relation to the life of grace. However, before we advance too far along, the genesis of the sacrament of the sick in God's plan of salvation needs to be further drawn forth.

From the Old Testament through the New Testament, care and ministry to the sick and dying is a constitutive component of God's plan for human salvation. Psalm 34, to provide one example, offers a great witness of faith in God for those in trouble or in need of deliverance:

I will bless the LORD at all times;
    his praise shall continually be in my mouth.
My soul makes its boast in the LORD;
    let the humble hear and be glad. . . .

I sought the Lord, and he answered me,
  and delivered me from all my fears. . . .
This poor man cried, and the Lord heard him,
  and saved him out of all his troubles.
The angel of the Lord encamps
  around those who fear him, and delivers them.
O taste and see that the Lord is good!
  Blessed is the man who takes refuge in him!
O fear the Lord, you his saints,
  for those who fear him have no want!
The young lions suffer want and hunger;
  but those who seek the Lord lack no good thing. . . .

What man is there who desires life,
  and covets many days, that he may enjoy good? . . .
The eyes of the Lord are toward the righteous,
  and his ears toward their cry.
The face of the Lord is against evildoers,
  to cut off the remembrance of them from the earth
When the righteous cry for help, the Lord hears,
  and delivers them out of all their troubles.
The Lord is near to the brokenhearted,
  and saves the crushed in spirit.

Many are the afflictions of the righteous;

but the LORD delivers him out of them
all.
He keeps all his bones;
   not one of them is broken. . . .
The LORD redeems the life of his servants;
   none of those who take refuge in him
will be condemned.

The revelation that God never abandons the lowly or the suffering, even when there is no apparent escape from destruction, is a basic tenet of the Christian faith. Isaiah 53 clarifies how God will send a suffering servant, a man of sorrows, to carry the burdens of the faithful and redeem them from loss by his own travails. This text is pivotal for the Church's understanding of how Christ's own suffering and redemptive mission fulfills God's plan and continues his ministry to the destitute. Isaiah proclaims: "Surely he has borne our griefs and carried our sorrows; . . . upon him was the chastisement that made us whole, and with his stripes we are healed . . . by his knowledge shall the righteous one, my servant, make many to be accounted righteous; and he shall bear their iniquities" (53:4–5, 11). Many more passages from the Old Testament professing faith in God's protection especially for the poor and afflicted could be cited, but the main point is simple: God is ever faithful to his promises, always near to those who are helpless, and able to redeem his children from every situation, even if there is no apparent avenue for escape or deliverance.

It is precisely the act of trusting in God, even when it seems like the enemy has triumphed, that marks off Judeo-Christian faith from pagan idolatry, scientism, utopian political ideology, and the dystopian views of atheistic existentialism. The just do not place their hope in anyone or anything but God. The *Catechism* explains this attitude of biblical faith:

> The man of the Old Testament lives his sickness in the presence of God. It is before God that he laments his illness, and it is of God, Master of life and death, that he implores healing. Illness becomes a way to conversion; God's forgiveness initiates the healing. It is the experience of Israel that illness is mysteriously linked to sin and evil, and that faithfulness to God according to his law restores life: "For I am the Lord, your healer." The prophet intuits that suffering can also have a redemptive meaning for the sins of others. Finally Isaiah announces that God will usher in a time for Zion when he will pardon every offense and heal every illness.[5]

The Old Testament background is important for understanding Christ's own life and saving mission. The faith of the just in the redeeming power of God is brought to fulfillment in the New Testament revelation of God's love for humanity in Christ. Christ is, quite literally, the incarnation in human form of God's love for humankind, especially for the sick and suffering. "Christ's compas-

---

[5] *CCC*, 1502.

sion toward the sick," the *Catechism* teaches,

> and his many healings of every kind of
> infirmity are a resplendent sign that "God
> has visited his people" and that the King-
> dom of God is close at hand. Jesus has the
> power not only to heal, but also to forgive
> sins; he has come to heal the whole man,
> soul and body; he is the physician the sick
> have need of. His compassion toward all
> who suffer goes so far that he identifies
> himself with them: "I was sick and you
> visited me." His preferential love for the
> sick has not ceased through the centuries
> to draw the very special attention of Chris-
> tians toward all those who suffer in body
> and soul. It is the source of tireless efforts
> to comfort them.[6]

In his ministry, Christ clarifies that the principal
gift he brings to the world is the full and complete healing of the human person—the forgiveness of sins. In Christ, God does not merely heal
our external wounds. Rather, he justifies or makes
right all the way down to the heart and soul of his
followers. The Christian Scriptures emphasize that
the primary illness every human being suffers from
is sin and its effects. Sometimes Christ confirms
his spiritual gifts—the forgiveness of sins—with
physical healings, but the physical healings are not
his primary gift. They confirm the deeper, more
hidden gift of forgiveness. This is especially evi-

---

[6] *CCC*, 1503.

dent in the account of the healing of the paralytic in Mark 2:5–12:

> And when Jesus saw their faith, he said to the paralytic, "Child, your sins are forgiven." Now some of the scribes were sitting there, questioning in their hearts, "Why does this man speak thus? It is blasphemy! Who can forgive sins but God alone?" And immediately Jesus, perceiving in his spirit that they questioned like this within themselves, said to them, "Why do you question like this in your hearts? Which is easier, to say to the paralytic, 'Your sins are forgiven,' or to say, 'Rise, take up your pallet and walk'? But that you may know that the Son of man has authority on earth to forgive sins"—he said to the paralytic—"I say to you, rise, take up your pallet and go home." And he rose, and immediately took up the pallet and went out before them all; so that they were all amazed and glorified God, saying, "We never saw anything like this!"

As this passage indicates, Christ's healings "announced a more radical healing: the victory over sin and death through his Passover. On the cross Christ took upon himself the whole weight of evil and took away the 'sin of the world,' of which illness is only a consequence."[7] Furthermore, as Mary Healy observes in her commentary on Mark's

---

[7] *CCC*, 1505.

Gospel, Jesus's response to the paralytic, "Child, your sins are forgiven," reveals a deeper insight into the human condition than what his audience is expecting—namely, "the interior crippling that comes from sin."[8] The same commentator goes on to observe some key additional points:

> In linking illness with sin, Jesus is drawing on a biblical theme familiar to his listeners: although illness is contrary to God's intention, it is one of the evils that afflict humanity as a consequence of sin. . . . This does not mean that all illness can be directly attributed to personal fault; the examples of Job and the suffering of the just man in the Psalms show that the innocent also suffer. But in this case Jesus evidently sees into this man's heart and releases him from a burden of guilt that he has borne, perhaps unconsciously, for years. It is the precondition to his being freed of his physical handicap.[9]

Christ's saving mission and ministry to the sick is more than just an arbitrary series of physical healings. The Christian faith offers the sick and dying much more than mere optimism that God might give a miracle. Christ's mission transforms the fallen world all the way down to the sinful disorders of the human heart. Indeed, Christ presents himself and his ministry in healing categories to

---

[8] Mary Healy, *The Gospel of Mark*, Catholic Commentary on Sacred Scripture (Grand Rapids, MI: Baker Academic, 2008), 56.

[9] Healy, *The Gospel of Mark*, 56–57.

draw out this point. He is a physician who brings complete healing to those in need: "And Jesus answered them, 'Those who are well have no need of a physician, but those who are sick; I have not come to call the righteous, but sinners to repentance'" (Luke 5:31–32). Christ identifies himself as the physician who has both the power and wisdom to meet the needs of our sinful human condition, which go well beyond the ailments that afflict the body. Christ's resurrection, Mary's bodily assumption into heaven, and the promise of our own bodily resurrection demonstrate that Christ's lordship will ultimately establish a complete eschatological restoration of fallen creation and human life.

How God's care for the sick, especially in Christ, concretely intersects with the Sacrament of Anointing of the Sick is hinted at by the Second Council of Lyons in 1274. The profession of faith issued by this council mentions all seven sacraments and the apostolic origin of Anointing of the Sick:

> The same Holy Roman Church also holds and teaches that there are seven sacraments of the Church: one is baptism . . . another is the sacrament of confirmation, which bishops confer by the laying on of hands while they anoint the reborn; then penance, the Eucharist, the sacrament of orders, matrimony, and *extreme unction [anointing of the sick], which, according to the doctrine of the Blessed James, is administered to the sick.*[10]

---

[10] Henrich Denzinger, *Compendium of Creeds, Definitions, and*

The seven sacraments that Christ instituted provide causal links between the life of the Church and the risen Christ. The sacraments are spiritual medicine that Christ administers to bring about the full healing and restoration of the human race. When he ascended into heaven, Christ did not rob the world of his healing ministry. Rather, by instituting seven sacraments in the Church that he founded and by pouring out his Spirit upon the Church from his heavenly throne, Christ carried on his saving mission. God's plan of salvation is now continued by the risen Christ through the sacramental life of the Church.

The doctrine of "Blessed James" mentioned in the excerpt above from Lyons II refers to a famous passage in the New Testament found in chapter 5 of the Letter of James. The Church draws upon this passage in her teaching on the Anointing of the Sick. In this passage, James testifies to the Church's practice of a rite of priestly anointing of the sick with oil:

> Is any among you sick? Let him call for the elders of the Church, and let them pray over him, anointing him with oil in the name of the Lord; and the prayer of faith will save the sick man, and the Lord will raise him up; and if he has committed sins, he will be forgiven. Therefore confess your sins to one another, and pray for one another, that you may be healed. (Jas 5:14–16)

Declarations on Matters of Faith and Morals, 43rd ed., ed. Peter Hünermann (San Francisco: Ignatius Press, 2012), 283 (§860). Emphasis added.

This passage outlines all of the components of a well-established sacramental rite in the Church:

1. The eligible recipient is identified: the sick.
2. The minister is identified: an "elder." The Greek word for "elders" used in this passage is *presbyters*, which is the term for "priest." The passage was translated into Latin as *presbyteros ecclesiae* [priests of the Church].
3. A form of the rite is identified: the priest will "pray . . . in the name of the Lord" over the sick.
4. The sacramental matter is indicated: "anointing [the sick person] with oil."
5. Several effects are produced by the rite: "the prayer of faith will save the sick man," "the Lord will raise him up," and "if he has committed sins, he will be forgiven."

This passage from James 5, in short, demonstrates the understanding within the early Church of the presence of a special sacramental rite for sick Christians administered by priests with special prayers and anointing with oil. There is a clear eschatological sense of this passage: the "Lord" works through the rite to "raise up" the recipient; the healing offered in the sacrament, like Christ's words in Mark 2 ("my son, your sins are forgiven"), is ordered to the forgiveness of sins and salvation.

James uses the word "save" a number of times in this epistle, and his usage always implies eschatological salvation, not merely physical "healing" from an illness. For example, in 1:21 James instructs us to "put away all filthiness and rank growth of wickedness and receive with meekness the implanted word, which is able to save your souls." Likewise, in the well-known faith-works passage in James 2:14, we find "What does it profit, my brethren, if a man says he has faith but has not works? Can his faith save him?" Thus in 5:14 when the effect of the priestly anointing given to the sick is described—"the prayer of faith will *save* the sick man, and the Lord will raise him up"—it is evident that the salvation associated with this rite, in the mind of James, is eschatological—healing in relation to sin—and not merely a cure for a physical illness. As Colman O'Neill observes commenting on this passage, "Christ has it in his power to restore bodily health; but the only certain promise that he had made about it is that he will bring final bodily resurrection."[11]

Furthermore, while this passage does not explicitly categorize the degree of illness or proximity to death that the "sick" person be in, the passage does imply that the ailment is serious. John Kasza explains:

> Most commentators see in the letter from James an implicit (but strong) indication that the subject is seriously ill and unable to go to the presbyters; hence, they (the elders) need to visit the sick person. . . .

---

[11] Colman E. O'Neill, O.P., *Sacramental Realism: A General Theory of the Sacraments* (Chicago: Midwest Theological Forum, 1998), 202.

Clearly, the author of the letter has in mind
a person who is dangerously ill, not someone who merely has a cold.[12]

The connection between God's fidelity as
redeemer, Christ's healing ministry, and the sacramental life of the Church is sometimes forgotten today. However, the faith and teachings of the
Church have always held these realities closely
together. The rite of Anointing of the Sick encap-
sulates and continues God's concern for the sick
and the suffering in the Old Testament and Christ's
ministry of healing and forgiveness in the New
Testament. The power of God's mercy toward the
sick and the suffering is continued and extended in
the life of the Church, especially through the rite
of the Sacrament of Anointing of the Sick.

In fact, as early as Mark 6 we find Christ
including anointing the sick with oil in the Apostles' mission:

> And he called to him the Twelve, and
> began to send them out two by two, and
> gave them authority over the unclean spir-
> its. He charged them to take nothing for
> their journey except a staff; no bread, no
> bag, no money in their belts; but to wear
> sandals and not put on two tunics. And he
> said to them, "Where you enter a house,
> stay there until you leave the place. And
> if any place will not receive you and they

---

[12] John C. Kasza, *Understanding Sacramental Healing: Anointing
and Viaticum* (Chicago: Hillenbrand Books, 2007), 20.

refuse to hear you, when you leave, shake off the dust that is on your feet for a testimony against them." So they went out and preached that men should repent. *And they cast out many demons, and anointed with oil many that were sick and healed them.* (Mark 6:7–13; emphasis added)

Scholars are divided as to whether or not this particular sending forth of the Apostles to anoint the sick with oil is an explicit reference to Christ's institution of the sacrament of the sick or merely a general commission to care for the sick in the nonsacramental way. "This is the only time in the Gospels," Mary Healy notes, "that anointing with oil is mentioned in conjunction with curing the sick, although it later becomes a practice of the early Church (James 5:14). Oil was used for medicinal purposes (Luke 10:34), but here its sacramental value as a vehicle for divine healing is emphasized."[13]

Pope Paul VI, following the teaching of the Council of Trent, explains the institution of this sacrament by distinguishing its "allusion" in Christ's mandate in Mark 6 and "promulgation" in James 5: "It was instituted by Christ and that it is 'alluded to in Mark (Mk 6:13) and recommended and promulgated to the faithful by James the apostle and brother of the Lord.'"[14] The Church, there-

---

[13] Healy, *The Gospel of Mark*, 117.

[14] Pope Paul VI, *Sacram Unctione Infirmorum: On the Sacrament of Anointing of the Sick* (November 13, 1972), http://www.vatican.va/content/paul-vi/en/apost_constitutions/documents/hf_p-vi_apc_19721130_sacram-unctionem.html.

fore, continues God's care of the sick and Christ's ministry of healing and salvation to the sick by means of the celebration of the sacramental rite of Anointing of the Sick. It is correct to say that Jesus himself continues his ministry of healing through the Church's sacramental rite. Jesus was deeply committed to showing mercy to the sick and the suffering. He joined the ministry of his Apostles to his own concern for the sick, which is carried out now in the Church, especially through the Sacrament of Anointing of the Sick. In fact, because of Christ's presence in the sacramental rites of the Church, the Second Vatican Council declared that "every liturgical celebration, because it is an action of Christ the priest and of His Body which is the Church, is a sacred action surpassing all others; no other action of the Church can equal its efficacy by the same title and to the same degree."[15]

This rite is not a hollow piece of ceremony or therapeutic consolation but a proclamation and application of the power of the Word of God and the message of the Gospel to those in most need of God's assistance.[16] Christ instituted the sacrament

---

[15] Second Vatican Council, *Sacrosanctum Concilium*, in *Decrees of the Ecumenical Councils*, vol. 2, *Trent to Vatican II*, ed. Norman P. Tanner, S.J. (Washington, D.C.: Georgetown University Press, 1990), §7.4.

[16] Both Luther and Calvin reject the inclusion of Anointing of the Sick among the sacraments instituted by the Lord. Both fail to see the sacramental continuity in practice between Mark 6 and James 5 and the use of the rite in the life of the early Church. Both also reject the text of James 5 as indicating an established sacramental rite. Neither, however, offers satisfactory accounts of the Church's reception of James 5 and Anointing of the Sick as a sacramental practice. For Martin

of the sick so that he could maintain his close proximity to and care for the sick from heaven through the sacramental ministry of the Church:

> Christ invites his disciples to follow him by taking up their cross in their turn. By following him they acquire a new outlook on illness and the sick. Jesus associates them with his own life of poverty and service. He makes them share in his ministry of compassion and healing: "So they went out and preached that men should repent. And they cast out many demons, and anointed with oil many that were sick and healed them."[17]

In order to appreciate fully the merciful gift of this sacrament and the grace it causes, it is necessary to consider the human condition in light of the effects that original and personal sin have on every person. Especially in the modern world, it

---

Luther's treatment of Anointing of the Sick, see his *Pagan Servitude of the Church* (Babylonian Captivity), nos. 184–92 in *Martin Luther*, ed. John Dillenberger (New York: Anchor Books, 1961), 351–56. For John Calvin's treatment, see book IV, nos. 18–21 of his *Institutes of the Christian Religion*, vol. 2, trans. Henry Beveridge (London: James Clarke and Co., 1962), 636–38. As Bernhard Poschmann points out, neither Luther nor Calvin recognizes the significance of James's reference to the anointing being done "in the name of the Lord." Elsewhere in the New Testament, this phrase is used for sacramental acts such as Baptism (see Acts 19:5). See Bernhard Poschmann, *Penance and Anointing of the Sick*, trans. Francis Courtney (New York: Herder and Herder, 1964), 236.

[17] *CCC*, 1506.

is not clear why Christ's desire to fully heal every human being all the way down to the heart is more redemptive than a miraculous bodily healing. As a result, some diagnosis of the human condition is necessary.

Original Sin, the Human Condition, and the Spiritual Significance of Anointing of the Sick

What is the point of the gift of sacramental healing—healing in the order of grace? Human beings do not live in a concrete order in which sin, suffering, and imperfection are reducible to bad moral patterns and unjust social structures, as if the world and each person are born in a state of spiritual and bodily integrity and then fall into corruption through bad choices or social injustice. Though there is genuine insight in the proverbial wisdom that money is the root of evil, the world's problems cannot be reduced to structural injustice alone, nor can they be solved solely through the establishment of material equality. Rather, the Christian faith clarifies that the concrete state of the world itself and the human condition is the result of a more fundamental disorder. This disorder is the consequence of the sin of the human race's first parents, Adam and Eve. This first sin is explained in chapter 3 of the Book of Genesis as a disregard for the order and limits placed on human freedom and knowledge by God:

> And the woman said to the serpent, "We may eat of the fruit of the trees of the

> garden; but God said, 'You shall not eat of
> the fruit of the tree which is in the midst
> of the garden, neither shall you touch it,
> lest you die.'" But the serpent said to the
> woman, "You will not die. For God knows
> that when you eat of it your eyes will be
> opened, and you will be like God, knowing
> good and evil." (Gen 3:2–5)

Notice that the antithesis of being alive with the
breath of God is contained in the end result of
sin, of disobeying God—namely, death. To turn
away from God by sinning is to turn away from the
source of life. The pursuit of godlike knowledge by
Adam and Eve against the order of life established
by God inaugurates a new age in creation, in which
the result of life without God plays itself out in
the consequent disorder of nature and the human
condition. In Genesis 3:16–19, the disorder within
creation resulting from the Fall that human beings
will experience is narrated by God himself:

> To the woman he said,
> "I will greatly multiply your pain in child-
> bearing;
>   in pain you shall bring forth children,
> yet your desire shall be for your husband,
>   and he shall rule over you."
> And to Adam he said,
> "Because you have listened to the voice of
> your wife,
>   and have eaten of the tree
> of which I commanded you,
>   'You shall not eat of it,'

cursed is the ground because of you;
     in toil you shall eat of it all the days of
your life;
thorns and thistles it shall bring forth to
you;
     and you shall eat the plants of the field.
In the sweat of your face
     you shall eat bread
till you return to the ground,
     for out of it you were taken;
you are dust,
     and to dust you shall return."

The Fall, therefore, introduces a condition of life and state of existence that is bereft of the original spiritual gift of life. This new fallen state that includes bodily death is known by the Christian tradition as the state of "original sin." In this state, the original harmony of life that God had established by elevating the gift of natural life with his presence in creation through the gift of grace was lost. Prior to the Fall, human beings were not disordered within themselves or between each other, creation was not hostile to them, and God was an integral part of their lives. After the Fall, life on earth becomes more difficult; it includes bodily pain, strife between the sexes, manual labor and food production become excessively laborious, and human life ultimately ends in biological death: "you are dust, and to dust you shall return" (Gen 3:19).

It is important to recall that prior to the Fall, at the end of Genesis 2 (v. 25), "the man and his wife" are described as being "naked" and "not ashamed." This enigmatic reference to Adam and Eve's life prior to the Fall alludes to a state of complete harmony between body and soul. In contrast, in Genesis 3:8, just after the Fall, when God appears in the Garden, we are told that Adam and Eve "heard the sound of the LORD God walking in the garden in the cool of the day, and the man and his wife hid themselves from the presence of the LORD God among the trees of the garden." Sin had moved creation and the condition of Adam and Eve from a state of harmony (being without shame) to a state of disorder (hiding from God) resulting in death.

The loss of harmony is played out uniquely in human beings, whose biological life is informed and elevated by the spiritual principal of the immortal soul and its powers. The spiritual component—the God-breathed soul—is a distinguishing mark of human life. It is a basic tenet of the Christian faith that one of the aspects of the state of original justice that was thrown into disorder by the Fall is that "the control of the soul's spiritual faculties over the body is shattered."[18] As a result, rather than live an embodied life animated, ordered, and guided by means of the spiritual faculties of the rational soul, human beings must now struggle to properly guide and regulate the inclinations of the body under the direction of the soul according to a measure consistent with their original purposes. "The doctrine of original sin," the *Catechism* teaches,

---

[18] *CCC*, 400.

closely connected with that of redemption by Christ, provides lucid discernment of man's situation and activity in the world. By our first parents' sin, the devil has acquired a certain domination over man, even though man remains free. Original sin entails "captivity under the power of him who thenceforth had the power of death, that is, the devil." Ignorance of the fact that man has a wounded nature inclined to evil gives rise to serious errors in the areas of education, politics, social action and morals.[19]

This is why the imperfection so manifest in ourselves, in the world around us, and in all of human history is not merely the result of recurring patterns of economic injustice. Human nature itself is wounded; every human being is thus wounded and in need of redemption. As the Second Vatican Council affirms:

> Therefore man is split within himself. As a result, all of human life, whether individual or collective, shows itself to be a dramatic struggle between good and evil, between light and darkness. Indeed, man finds that by himself he is incapable of battling the assaults of evil successfully, so that everyone feels as though he is bound by chains. But the Lord Himself came to free and strengthen man, renewing him inwardly

---

[19] *CCC*, 407.

and casting out that "prince of this world" (John 12:31) who held him in the bondage of sin. For sin has diminished man, blocking his path to fulfillment.[20]

This struggle to harmonize the life of the body under the direction of the powers of the soul is experienced by every human being, even when health and bodily life is flourishing. Moral vices like anger, greed, envy, gluttony, and lust—vices that flow from the heart—clearly indicate that there is an interior ailment in every human person that is in need of healing. The additional struggle caused by this ailment or wound plays out especially in end-of-life situations, when the body is weak due to illness and the person suffers from physical and emotional fatigue.

This state of disorder is a universal condition, inherited by all members of the human race from the Fall of its first parents. In Genesis 1:28, prior to the Fall, God blesses Adam and Eve and says, "Be fruitful and multiply, and fill the earth and subdue it." After the Fall, however, what Adam and Eve multiplied through the transmission of life was their fallen state, in which, lacking the extra spiritual dynamism of God's breath—the gift of grace—the soul is not able to harmonize bodily movements and passions or sustain the body from natural corruption and death. St. Paul clearly affirms the universal inheritance of Adam and Eve's post-lapse condition in Romans 5 when he compares the Fall of all human

---

[20] Second Vatican Council, *Gaudium et Spes* (December 7, 1965), §13.

beings in "Adam" to the redemption of each human being in Christ:

> Therefore as sin came into the world through one man and death through sin, and so death spread to all men because all men sinned. . . . But the free gift is not like the trespass. For if many died through one man's trespass, much more have the grace of God and the free gift in the grace of that one man Jesus Christ abounded for many. . . . Then as one man's trespass led to condemnation for all men, so one man's act of righteousness leads to acquittal and life for all men. For as by one man's disobedience many were made sinners, so by one man's obedience many will be made righteous. (Rom 5:12, 15, 18–19)

In short, the state of original justice with its harmony and order was the condition of the human race that God blessed and intended Adam and Eve to share with their posterity. What they actually transmitted, however, was a fallen condition alienated from God—wounded—with bodily disorders and mortality resulting from the effects of sin. Original sin is inherited from Adam and Eve because it is the condition, after the Fall, that is transmitted to their descendants.

The disordered state resulting from the Fall is recognized by the Christian tradition to include both moral and physical types of evil. Moral evil includes the faults committed by human beings. Physical evil describes the things that happen to us, such as illness and natural disaster. The imperfections and struggles of both the moral and physical order that all humans experience in the world are the result of the state of disorder inaugurated by the Fall; they are not some type of ongoing vengeance inflicted upon us by a vindictive God. As the *Catechism* teaches:

> Although it is proper to each individual, *original sin does not have the character of a personal fault in any of Adam's descendants.* It is a deprivation of original holiness and justice, but human nature has not been totally corrupted: it is wounded in the natural powers proper to it, subject to ignorance, suffering and the dominion of death, and inclined to sin—an inclination to evil that is called "concupiscence." Baptism, by imparting the life of Christ's grace, erases original sin and turns a man back towards God, but the consequences for nature, weakened and inclined to evil, persist in man and summon him to spiritual battle.[21]

In fact, in John 9:2 the Apostles ask Jesus whose sins are responsible for a man's blindness, the sins of the man himself or his parents. In response, Jesus states that the man's blindness was not the result of his own or his parents' sins: the physical evil of blindness is not a penalty imposed by God for some wrongdoing on the part of the afflicted man or those close to him. The man's blindness is a result of original sin.

---

[21] *CCC*, 405. Emphasis added.

Suffering raises some common and understandable questions: "How could God have created a world with so much suffering and death?" "If God truly loves me, then why am I afflicted with this illness?" It should be recognized that it is perhaps those in an end-of-life situation, or their loved ones, whose faith is most acutely challenged by the existence of evil and suffering in the world. Though not magically erasing the reality of suffering and death, the Church's teaching on original sin and redemption in Christ offers much consolation to those confronted with the effects of sin in the world. The doctrines of the Fall and original sin remind us of important truths in relation to these types of questions: God did not create a world filled with sin, suffering, and death. God created the world in a state of perfect harmony and fullness of life in which death and disorder had no part. Death and disorder are not the products of God's creative activity, but rather the result of our first parents turning away from the original plan for human life on earth. The Book of Wisdom famously declares (1:12–14; emphasis added): "Do not invite death by the error of your life, nor bring on destruction by the works of your hands; *because God did not make death*, and he does not delight in the death of the living."

People who are facing their own death or the death of a loved one, or those caring for someone who is dying, can feel as though they are the victims of God's anger or abandonment. It is important to remind them that the current order and state is not the original gift that God gave to humanity. Fortunately, however, even though God did not "make death," it is also the case that humanity's current fallen and wounded state is not outside of God's providential order and care for all things. Indeed, the whole message of the Gospel is one of redemption from the tragedy, disorder, and loss of the Fall.

Human beings need to understand themselves, their struggles, and the world around them in light of the effects of sin so they can recognize that their mortality is not a wrathful punishment, and so they can accept the need that each person has for redemption by God from this condition. While the disquiet associated with the problem of evil is wholly understandable, the problem of evil would only be an insoluble problem if God had no plan or solution to redeem us from evil.

The sick and their loved ones also need to be reminded that the effects of sin and evil in the world do not have the last word. St. Paul powerfully reminds us in Romans 8 that none of the terrible things that happen in this life are more powerful than God's love for us in Christ:

> What then shall we say to this? If God is for us, who is against us? He who did not spare his own Son but gave him up for us all, will he not also give us all things with him? Who shall bring any charge against God's elect? It is God who justifies; who is to condemn? Is it Christ Jesus, who died, yes, who was raised from the dead, who is at the right hand of God, who indeed intercedes for us? Who shall separate us from the love of Christ? Shall tribulation, or distress, or persecution, or famine, or nakedness, or

peril, or sword? As it is written, "For your sake we are being killed all the day long; we are regarded as sheep to be slaughtered." *No, in all these things we are more than conquerors through him who loved us. For I am sure that neither death, nor life, nor angels, nor principalities, nor things present, nor things to come, nor powers, nor height, nor depth, nor anything else in all creation, will be able to separate us from the love of God in Christ Jesus our Lord.* (Rom 8:31–39; emphasis added)

It is of paramount importance for ministers, health care workers, and any other caregivers to remind those facing death that there is no power in the world, even death itself, that can separate a human being from the love of God. The post-Fall condition of the world and the human race is indeed one of trial and challenge, but the message of the Gospel teaches that God has redeemed humanity from this condition. The purpose of the Sacrament of Anointing of the Sick is to deepen the power of Christ's redemption in those who are passing from this life so that they may die fully united to God in Christ Jesus and live in eternal union with him in the next life.

The Twofold Aspect of Death

The first sin of Adam and Eve, and analogously all the personal sins committed by each human being, causes a twofold death. The first death is of the spiritual order. It consists in the loss of God's presence in the soul by grace. This spiritual death is also related to the second death, which is the physical death of the body. The presence of God in the soul through grace is described by spiritual writers as a light or flame by which the life of God shines within us, healing and elevating our natures and natural capacities to supernatural union with him. As Paul teaches in Romans 5:5, "God's love has been poured into our hearts through the Holy Spirit who has been given to us." Because of this gift, this infusion of God's presence within the human soul, Paul reminds Christians of their spiritual and bodily dignity: "Do you not know that your body is a temple of the Holy Spirit within you, which you have from God? You are not your own; you were bought with a price. So glorify God in your body" (1 Cor 6:19–20).

This hidden, interior light is present within each believer who is in the state of grace. As the presence of God within us, grace elevates and orients the powers and faculties of the soul, uniting them with God, through the habits of faith, hope, and charity and the assistance of the gifts of the Holy Spirit and the beatitudes. Grace is a new life in the soul elevating our fallen state. This is why Adam and Eve's loss in Eden is referred to as the "Fall." They fell to a state of corruption from the elevated state of union that they previously had with God by grace. Original sin and personal sin leave human nature wounded and devoid of the aid of God's presence within the soul. Redemption in Christ works to restore, heal, and elevate the "image of God" that sin wounds and defaces. The current state of life that every human being is born into is one that lacks this higher principle of life: grace.

As a result, after the Fall, the tendency to sin is especially strong in relation to those things that bring bodily comfort and pleasure. St. Paul personifies and personalizes this tendency to sin within each human being in a powerful description of his own struggles: "So I find it be a law that when I want to do right, evil lies close at hand. For I delight in the law of God, in my inmost self, but I see in my members another law at war with the law of my mind and making me captive to the law of sin which dwells in my members" (Rom 7:21–23). This tension within each human being between the healing and sanctification of grace, which incline to spiritual realities, and the tendency to sin, which attaches to material things, plays out in a particular way, as Thomas Aquinas explains:

> Now man is placed between the things of this world, and spiritual goods wherein eternal happiness consists: so that the more he cleaves to the one, the more he withdraws from the other, and conversely. Wherefore he that cleaves wholly to the things of this world, so as to make them his end, and to look upon them as the reason and rule of all he does, falls away altogether from spiritual goods.[22]

---

[22] Thomas Aquinas, *ST* I-II, q. 108, a. 4. Taken from Thomas Aquinas, *Summa theologiae*, vol. 16, ed. John Mortensen and Enrique Alarcón, trans. Laurence Shapcote, O.P. (Lander, WY: The Aquinas Institute for the Study of Sacred Doctrine, 2012), 434–35.

This struggle is something that all human beings, including followers of Christ, experience within themselves. It is easy to think of each particular sin as a transient action that has no abiding impact on the moral, spiritual, or bodily life of the one who commits it. However, as St. Paul reminds the Romans, though God's free gift of grace leads to "eternal life in Christ Jesus our Lord," the life of sin also pays out negative rewards, as "the wages of sin is death" (Rom 6:23).

Thus, there are two ways of living: there is life according to the disorders of the flesh, which feeds the fallen and disordered appetites for destruction, and there is life according to the spirit, made possible by Christ's saving work and the outpouring of the Holy Spirit elevating the soul to union with God. The life according to the spirit lives for God and the things of God, not for the gratification of the sinful longings of the flesh. "For those who live according to the flesh set their minds on the things of the flesh," Paul teaches in Romans 8:5–8, "but those who live according to the Spirit set their minds on the things of the Spirit. To set the mind on the flesh is death, but to set the mind on the Spirit is life and peace. For the mind that is set on the flesh is hostile to God; it does not submit to God's law, indeed it cannot; and those who are in the flesh cannot please God."

These basic points of Christian anthropology, of sin and its consequences, are very important for understanding the gift that Christ wishes to bestow in Anointing of the Sick. The twofold death that sin causes makes life a battle, even for the believer. Sin is not just a spiritual ailment; it also impacts bodily life and existence. The gift of grace heals the soul and brings forgiveness, but the bodily impact of sin remains, leaving the believer vulnerable to recurring inclinations to sinful behavior or weakness. In the early Church the doctrine of "deadly sins" was developed to underscore the fact that sinful actions can become vicious habits. As Robert Fastiggi notes:

> Sins engaged in freely and repetitively inevitably result in "perverse inclinations, which cloud conscience and corrupt the concrete judgment of good and evil" (CCC, 1865). These perverse inclinations to sin can also be called vices, which are habits that "have arisen through the repetition of acts." Following St. John Cassian (c. 360–433) and St. Gregory the Great (c. 540–604), Church tradition has emphasized seven capital sins or vices; they are called "capital" because "they engender other sins, other vices" (CCC, 1866). These seven sins or vices are pride, avarice, envy, wrath, lust, gluttony, and sloth (or *acedia*).[23]

This reality is especially evident when it comes to sins of excess like gluttony. Someone can wake up from a night of hard drinking or excess eating and be moved by guilt to confess their sins immediately. However, the bodily remnants of the fault, hangover or stomachache, can last even after for-

---

[23] Robert Fastiggi, *The Sacrament of Reconciliation: An Anthropological and Scriptural Understanding* (Chicago/Mundelein: Hillenbrand Books, 2017), 5.

giveness has been received. Addictive behaviors also drive home this point: individuals can quit cigarette smoking, drug use, or viewing pornography and yet continue to suffer habitually from the imprint that those behaviors leave within them for the remainder of their lives. Former smokers often feel an urge to smoke in certain situations or certain places, even years and decades after having kicked the habit.

The same is true for emotive and mental sins like anger, despair, jealousy, loneliness, pessimism, fear, and impatience. These habits are hard to break and frequently suggest themselves even though we wish to leave them behind. Contrasting Adam's condition before and after the Fall in relation to the benefit of Anointing of the Sick, Fr. Romanus Cessario explains:

> Adam with his preternatural human perfection lacked the beatific vision of God. Sinful Adam and his heirs find themselves further disadvantaged by reason of their attachment to sinful disorders and the "remains"—the *reliquiae*—that even forgiven sins leave on the soul and in the body. According to the ordinations of divine wisdom, each sacrament distinctly readies a believer for heavenly bliss by restoring and perfecting his or her Godly image.[24]

When we are especially vulnerable due to sick-

---

[24] Romanus Cessario, O.P., "Anointing of the Sick: The Sanctification of Human Suffering," *Nova et Vetera* 17, no. 2 (2019), 300.

ness or old age, these "remains" of sin more readily assault us. Even the most disciplined Christians realize that temptation is something to be expected as a regular part of the human journey to the last moment of our lives. In one of his famous "sayings" from the desert, the great Egyptian monk of the early Church offers the following advice to a fellow ascetic: "Abba Anthony said to Abba Poemen, 'this is the great work of a man: always to take the blame for his own sins before God and to expect temptation to his last breath.'"[25]

Anointing of the Sick is Christ's spiritual antidote to the bodily remnants of sin that remain in each human being. At death, the soul departs the body. However, if the remnants of sin weigh down or tie the soul to earthly attachments, it can be impeded from enjoying the spiritual delights that await it. "Because the soul is preparing for its immanent departure," John Boyle explains,

> it most especially needs to attend to those remains of sin that have served to weaken it and render it less than fit for glory. And so it is that this sacrament is not given against those defects by which the spiritual life is simply removed, namely original and mortal sin, but against those defects by which a man is spiritually weakened such that he has not the perfect vigor requisite for the acts of a life of grace and glory.[26]

---

[25] *The Sayings of the Desert Fathers*, trans. Benedicta Ward, S.L.G. (Trappist, KY: Cistercian Publications, 1984), no. 4, 2.

[26] John Boyle, "Saint Thomas Aquinas on the Anointing of the Sick," in *Rediscovering Aquinas and the Sacraments*, ed. Michael

Articulating the relationship between soul and body in terms that help people understand the unity of the human person is challenging. Some Christian thinkers use the metaphor of the impact that weather has on a body of water. A windy, raucous climate disturbs the water. So, too, the acts of the body can disturb the soul, and disordered movements of the soul can disturb the body. Father of the Church St. Gregory of Nyssa (d. 395) uses the example of a mirror:

> If, then, one should withdraw from those who seduce him to evil and by the use of his reason turn to the better, putting evil behind him, it is as if he places his own soul, like a mirror, face-to-face with the hope of good things, with the result that the images and impressions of virtue, as it is shown to him by God, are imprinted on the purity of his soul.[27]

Like a mirror, the soul reflects the things placed before it. In our earthly journey, it can be difficult to eradicate the reflections of the unholy things and actions to which we have subjected the soul. These sinful reflections weigh upon us, attach us to the world, and leave us vulnerable. By the grace of Anointing of the Sick, God faithfully and gently heals and strengthens against the bodily vices that may afflict those who are seriously ill.

Dauphinais and Matthew Levering (Chicago: Hillenbrand Books, 2009), 79.

[27] Gregory of Nyssa, *The Life of Moses*, trans. Abraham J. Malherbe (San Francisco: Harper San Francisco, 2006), 44.

Understanding Sin and Death: Why Is Life after Baptism So Difficult?

In John 3, Jesus explains to Nicodemus that Baptism constitutes a birth of new spiritual life that originates, like the life-giving spirit that God breathed into Adam, from heaven. In Romans 6, St. Paul explains that the symbolic aspect of Baptism connects the recipient to the death and resurrection of Christ. In Baptism, the sinful form of life that kills the spirit and alienates us from God—the life inherited from the Fall—is put to death, buried with Christ: "Do you not know," Paul asks in Romans (6:3–4), "that all of us who have been baptized into Christ Jesus were baptized into his death? We were buried therefore with him by baptism into death, so that as Christ was raised from the dead by the glory of the Father, we too might walk in newness of life." The regenerative grace of Baptism, Paul teaches, infuses a new spiritual life into the soul such that when we emerge from the waters of Baptism, a new life of grace is begun within us. Likewise, in Titus 3:4–8, Paul connects Baptism with new life, salvation, justification, and eternal life:

> When the goodness and loving kindness of God our Savior appeared, he saved us, not because of deeds done by us in righteousness, but in virtue of his own mercy, by the washing of regeneration and renewal in the Holy Spirit, which he poured out upon us richly through Jesus Christ our Savior, so that we might be justified by his grace and

become heirs in hope of eternal life. The saying is sure.

Because of the revealed teaching on Baptism as a death to sin and birth into a new life of the grace of the Holy Spirit, the Church teaches that "by Baptism all sins are forgiven, original sin and all personal sins, as well as all punishment for sin. In those who have been reborn nothing remains that would impede their entry into the Kingdom of God, neither Adam's sin, nor personal sin, nor the consequences of sin, the gravest of which is separation from God."[28]

Given this rich and hope-filled teaching about the new life and forgiveness communicated by the grace of Baptism, which is deepened by the other sacraments, especially the Eucharist, it is quite natural to wonder why it is that post-baptismal life entails so many spiritual and bodily challenges. If the Fall was a fall from grace—a spiritual death—and if the grace given in Baptism cleanses original sin and personal sin from the soul by a new infusion of grace, then why do the baptized struggle and suffer temptations? If the Holy Spirit is alive and active in the souls of believers by grace, elevating them to union with God, then why do they still suffer bodily weakness and death? These types of questions are both legitimate and unavoidable. In fact, given how challenging post-baptismal life can be, it could be tempting to think that Baptism and the other sacraments are perhaps empty and devoid of the power that Christians have attributed to them.

---

[28] *CCC*, 1263.

The differences between the condition in which Adam and Eve received grace prior to the Fall and the condition in which their descendants receive the grace of Baptism provide an answer to this problem. The grace and intimacy with God that Adam and Eve enjoyed before the Fall were bestowed upon integral human natures that had not been touched by sin. Prior to the Fall, the relationship between the body and soul, and between the individual and God, was fully harmonious. After the Fall, when anyone receives the graces of Baptism, they are receiving grace into human natures that have been touched by sin and its disorders. Just as a broken vase that has been glued back together is more susceptible to fracturing again and leaking along the old cracks that remain after it is put back together, so too each human person who is baptized receives grace in vessels that have been wounded and are in need of healing. In the fallen world, the healing received by the sacraments is progressive and ongoing. It is not fully realized until the resurrection of the body and the restoration of all things under Christ. The break of a bone can heal, and the function of the wounded area can return, but remnants and vulnerabilities of the old injury remain. "Certain temporal consequences of sin remain in the baptized," the *Catechism* explains,

> such as suffering, illness, death, and such frailties inherent in life as weaknesses of character, and so on, as well as an inclination to sin that Tradition calls *concupiscence*, or metaphorically, "the tinder for sin"

(*fomes peccati*); since concupiscence "is left for us to wrestle with, it cannot harm those who do not consent but manfully resist it by the grace of Jesus Christ." Indeed, "an athlete is not crowned unless he competes according to the rules."[29]

By dying on the Cross, Christ redeemed us from the eternal death caused by sin, but we must complete the temporal journey of this life in union with him in order to fully enjoy the fruits of his risen life in the next life. Eternal life is truly begun in Baptism, but it unfolds and deepens throughout the life of the Christian. The effect of the grace of Christ, Charles Journet observes, "is not, like that given to Adam, to eliminate but, since derived from Christ, to illuminate suffering and death. Jesus did not eliminate suffering and death for himself, but illuminated them; and the grace of the Redemption causes us to follow in his footsteps."[30]

---

[29] *CCC*, 1264.

[30] Charles Journet, *The Meaning of Grace*, trans. A. V. Littledale (Princeton: Scepter Publishers, 1996), 119.

CHAPTER III

THE SACRAMENT OF
ANOINTING OF THE SICK

The Need for a Sacrament of the Dying and Departing: Who Can Receive, and When?

Before we discuss the theology of the effects of Anointing of the Sick, it is important to clarify for whom Christ instituted this sacrament. Each sacrament of the Church is instituted for a specific spiritual purpose. Baptism, for example, is open to all of the unbaptized. Additionally, the recipients of subsequent sacraments, like Confirmation, Penance, and the Eucharist, have specific criteria that they must meet to be eligible to receive, such as being baptized, attaining a certain minimum age, having sins to confess in the case of Penance, not being in a state of mortal sin in the case of the Eucharist, and so on. To receive Holy Orders, for example, in addition to being sacramentally eligible (e.g., having been baptized and confirmed), one must also be a male.

There are necessary conditions for the reception of Anointing of the Sick, too. This sacrament, in particular, has been subject to abuse, perhaps well-intentioned, in regards to its administration. This abuse has contributed to a false perception of what Christ intends to accomplish in each recipient with this sacrament. For example, I was once at a parish that celebrated Anointing of the Sick on a fixed day each month after a Sunday Mass. At the end of the Mass, the priest announced that this was the Sunday for the celebration of Anointing of the Sick. He invited "anyone who is not feeling quite right" to stay after Mass and receive the sacrament.[1] This type of administration of the sacrament, however, is not only theologically and liturgically inaccurate, but it is also incredibly misleading and confusing for the faithful.[2] This sacrament is a type of medicine and healing related to the remnants that sin leaves on the body. It is to be given to the faithful at the time when those remnants of sin are especially difficult to overcome. Bodily infirmity, Thomas Aquinas observes, "at times . . . tends to hinder spiritual health: so far as bodily infirmity hinders the virtues. Therefore, it was suitable to employ some spiritual medicine against sin, in accord with the fact that bodily

---

[1] For a well-reasoned theological response to this misguided practice, see Levering, *Dying and the Virtues* (Grand Rapids, MI: William B. Eerdmans Publishing Company, 2018), 135–47.

[2] The Church teaches that "the practice of indiscriminately anointing numbers of people . . . simply because they are ill or have reach an advanced age is to be avoided" (*Pastoral Care of the Sick: Rites of Anointing and Viaticum* [Collegeville, MN: The Liturgical Press, 1983], 108).

infirmity flows out of sin. . . . And for this a sacrament was established—extreme unction."[3]

The Sacrament of Anointing of the Sick is thus not intended for those who are merely ill in the sense of being a bit off, having a cold or flu, and it is certainly not intended for those who are feeling off emotionally. Further, as Romanus Cessario points out, Christ's intention in instituting Anointing of the Sick was not as "the appropriate Catholic setting to offer a Christian-tinged form of psychological grief counseling."[4] The insertion of the Anointing of the Sick into life situations that are not related to serious illness and dying is misleading and spiritually harmful.

These abuses are often justified in the name of the teaching of the Second Vatican Council, with some asserting that the Council detached the administration of the sacrament from serious illness and end of life situations. Prior to Vatican II, Anointing of the Sick was spoken of as "Extreme Unction" (still a valid title for this sacrament) because the unction or anointing was the last sacramental anointing given to the sick "in extremis" or at the very outer limits of the dying process, often in close conjunction with the final moments of life. It is "extreme" because it is the last anointing received by a Christian. "Final anointing" is a very accurate translation of the Latin words

---

[3] Thomas Aquinas, *Summa contra gentiles*, book 4, *Salvation*, trans. Charles O'Neil (Notre Dame, IN: University of Notre Dame Press, 1957), 282–83 (chapter 73).

[4] Romanus Cessario, O.P., "Anointing of the Sick: The Sanctification of Human Suffering," *Nova et Vetera* 17, no. 2 (2019): 298.

for "extreme unction." Thomas Aquinas refers to Anointing of the Sick as "the sacrament of those departing."[5] The fourteenth session of the Council of Trent in 1551, following the previous tradition represented by Aquinas, clarifies for whom Christ instituted the sacrament of the sick in terms of their health condition vis-à-vis death: "This anointing is to be used for the sick, in particular those who are so dangerously ill that they seem about to depart from life; and consequently it is also called the sacrament of the departing."[6] Vatican II offers nothing to change the general trajectory of this teaching; in fact, the Council clearly affirms that this sacrament is for those who are in danger of death. The perception that the Council taught that the sacrament is not for those who are facing death due to sickness or old age is simply an urban legend that needs to be corrected in light of the clear teaching of the Church.

Vatican II does caution against the practice of waiting to administer the sacrament until the recipient's very last moments. As a result, the Council speaks of "Anointing of the Sick" instead of "extreme" anointing. However, the change in name and the administration of the sacrament earlier in the dying process in no way decouples the

---

5   Thomas Aquinas, *Commentary on the Sentences*, book IV, distinction 23, from *Commentary on the Sentences*, vol. 8, book IV, distinctions 14–25, trans. Beth Mortensen (Green Bay, WI: Aquinas Institute, Inc., 2017), 549.

6   Council of Trent, "Fourteenth Session," in *Decrees of the Ecumenical Councils*, vol. 2, *Trent to Vatican II*, ed. Norman P. Tanner, S.J. (Washington, D.C.: Georgetown University Press, 1990), 711.

sacrament from grave illness: "'Final anointing,' which can also and better be called 'anointing of the sick,' is not a sacrament exclusively for those who are involved in the final crisis of life and death. There can therefore be no doubt that *the point when a Christian begins to be in danger of death*, either through illness or old age, is already a suitable time to receive it."[7] The sacrament thus remains for those who are facing death. The Church now offers the sacrament to the sick earlier in the dying process so that they may benefit from its graces throughout their ordeal. It is still a final anointing for those in danger of departing from this life due to illness. This adjustment in the name and the timing of the administration of the sacrament was never intended to modify the basic tenet of faith that Christ instituted the sacrament for the gravely ill and those facing death.[8]

The position of the Church on this matter is clear as this passage from the *Catechism*, quoting Pope Paul VI following Vatican II, indicates: "The Anointing of the Sick 'is not a sacrament for those only who are at the point of death. Hence, *as soon*

---

[7] Second Vatican Council, *Sacrosanctum Concilium*, in *Decrees of the Ecumenical Councils*, vol. 2, *Trent to Vatican II*, ed. Norman P. Tanner, S.J. (Washington, D.C.: Georgetown University Press, 1990), §73. Italics added.

[8] For a careful theological critique of positions that assume Vatican II's change in language from "Extreme Unction" to "final anointing" or "Anointing of the Sick" implies that the Church now views the sacrament to be for healing more broadly construed and not, specifically, for the type of sacramental-eschatological healing that is needed to die well, see Levering, *Dying and the Virtues*, especially the notes on 277–80.

as anyone of the faithful begins to be in danger of death from sickness or old age, the fitting time for him to receive this sacrament has certainly already arrived.'"[9] So the Church does teach that the sacrament need not be administered merely "at the point of death." However, the Church also offers two conditions that the eligible recipient must meet: (1) they must have, at least, begun to be in danger of death, and (2) the danger of death must be due to sickness or old age. More will be said below about the condition of the recipient of the sacrament, but it should be clear that to be in proximity to death from an illness, the illness, by definition, is serious.

The point here should not be lost. Christians face many challenges and crises. "One of the principal crises which the Christian has to contend with is ill-health," Colman O'Neill explains. "When it is serious it needs more than the attention of a doctor; it is a crisis of the whole person, affecting his entire outlook."[10] Christ instituted this sacrament precisely for the sake of aiding dying Christians in this last crisis. The Church offers other resources to the faithful to aid them in other crises.

Isn't Everyone in Danger of Death?

All human beings are at least remotely in the pro-

---

[9]   *CCC*, 1514. Emphasis added. Note: By use of the term "faithful," this teaching presupposes that the recipient is a baptized Catholic, as do all sacraments received after Baptism.

[10] Colman E. O'Neill, *Meeting Christ in the Sacraments* (New York: Alba House, 1991), 281.

cess of dying. However, Anointing of the Sick is not for faithful who are suffering bad feelings, emotional instability, or some other danger not related to serious sickness or advanced age. This sacrament is not for those who are worried about dying or who might, for whatever reason, be a danger to themselves. This sacrament is for those who have a tangible proximity to death resulting from a serious ailment, an accident, or old age. Simply being sick, uncomfortable, down-and-out emotionally, or old does not mean that one has "begun" to be in danger of death or is departing from this life. There are many physical and emotional conditions that people can live with for a long time without dying from them.

Given that priests need sound judgment to determine whether or not someone who requests the sacrament is eligible, a highly developed pastoral prudence is required when administering Anointing of the Sick. A judgment to withhold the sacrament from someone who requests it will require a careful theological explanation. However, it is also extremely imprudent for pastors to offer the sacrament to those who have not "begun" to be in danger of death from sickness or age. In the same way that sins (that need to be confessed, over which one is contrite, for which one is willing to satisfy, and about which the priest may grant absolution) are the object of the Sacrament of Confession, so too the recipient of Anointing of the Sick must have an illness that places them in some proximity to death. It is precisely the sinful weakness of the body, exasperated by grave illness, that this sacrament is ordered to. Just as one without sins to confess cannot be granted absolution, so too one without serious bodily illness cannot receive the strengthening graces that this sacrament confers upon weaknesses. As Fr. Revel points out, this sacrament configures and conforms those suffering grave physical illness, in their very weakness, to Christ's own suffering and passion. The recipient of this sacrament must, therefore, be conformable to Christ's suffering and passion by way of a physical weakness approaching death.[11]

People who are not in danger of death due to sickness or old age should be directed to the other sacramental graces and spiritual practices that are open to all of the faithful, including Penance and frequent Communion, as well as the Bible and privileged devotional practices (like the Rosary) that nourish the spiritual life. They should also not replace care that they may need from professionals with the reception of Anointing of the Sick.

Discerning Danger of Death

Following long-standing Christian practice and tradition, common theological judgments, and sound pastoral prudence, the Roman Ritual provides examples to help clarify those who can be anointed:

---

[11] Jean-Philippe Revel, *Traité des sacrements*, vol. 6, *L'onction des maladies: Rédemption de la chair par la chair* (Paris: Éditions du Cerf, 2009), 193.

- "A sick person . . . before surgery whenever a serious illness is the reason for the surgery."
- "Elderly people . . . if they have become notably weakened even though no serious illness is present."
- "Sick children . . . if they have sufficient use of reason to be strengthened by the sacrament."
- "Sick people who, although they have lost consciousness or the use of reason, would, as Christian believers, probably have asked for it were they in control of their faculties."[12]

The Code of Canon Law gives ministers of the sacrament generous latitude to make judgments about bestowing the sacrament in cases of doubt: "This sacrament is to be administered when there is a doubt whether the sick person has attained the use of reason, whether the person is dangerously ill, or whether the person is dead."[13]

The Church's practice also looks to the distinction between internal and external threats to one's life to assess if a person is in need of Anointing of the Sick. This distinction goes as follows: Christ instituted the sacrament of the sick for those whose lives are threatened by a condition that is internal

---

[12] See *Pastoral Care of the Sick*, 13 [at §§9–12, 14].

[13] *The Code of Canon Law* (1983), https://www.vatican.va/archive/cod-iuris-canonici/cic_index_en.html, §1005. For a helpful and brief summary of the Church's canonical teaching on Anointing of the Sick, see Libero Gerosa, *Canon Law* (New York: Continuum, 2002), 167–74.

to them: serious sickness or old age. The sacrament is not to be administered to groups or to individuals because of an external threat to life such as war, natural disaster, crashing planes, sinking ships, or even the death penalty. Those whose lives are threatened by forces external to them can prepare for a possible death by recourse to Holy Communion, Confession, and other nonsacramental spiritual activities. People in these situations do not suffer the vulnerability of the remnants of sin that can inhibit the exercise of virtue when the body is in a weakened state. Anointing of the Sick is for the strengthening and consecration of those who face death as a result of the internal dissipation of biological life. The graces that this sacrament provides are ordered to ministering to the spiritual needs of someone suffering and dying as a result of an internal condition.[14]

Discerning Eligibility: Difficult Cases

The Dead and Unconscious

Regarding the liceity or appropriateness of administering the sacrament to those who have died prior to a priest being able to administer the sacrament, it is important to recall that scientific-medical criteria for death are circumscribed by empirical observations, such as cardiorespiratory indicators or brain activity. However, as noted above, human

---

[14] Paul Jerome Keller, O.P., *101 Questions & Answers on the Sacraments of Healing: Penance and Anointing of the Sick* (New York/Mahwah: Paulist Press, 2010), 110–11.

life is not reducible to biological categories: human life is animated by spiritual principles. As a result, the Church understands death to constitute more than the mere cessation of biological function. Death entails the separation of the soul from the body. As indicated by Christ's own words on the Cross—"Father, into your hands I commit my spirit" (Luke 23:46)—death is more than a physical phenomenon because the human person is a unity of body and soul.

Common sense indicates that the separation of soul and body happens in close conjunction with the cessation of biological functions. However, because the moment of the separation of the soul from the body cannot be empirically verified or strictly equated with bodily death, priests who reach a member of the faithful after they have been declared medically dead can still administer the sacrament. If the separation of soul and body has not taken place, the recipient could still benefit from the graces of the sacrament as they pass from this life to the next. Administering the sacrament to those who have been declared dead medically, of course, can be subject to abuse. The Church generally discourages the conferral of the sacrament on the deceased. Judging when it is no longer solemn and consistent with the dignity of the sacrament to administer it to someone who has passed also requires pastoral prudence. It is always possible to pray with the family of someone who has passed and to pray for the repose of the deceased without administering the sacrament.[15]

---

[15] For further commentary and a consideration of various sce-

When it comes to those who have lost the use of their mental faculties or who are alive but no longer conscious, the Church offers priests the following guideline: "This sacrament is to be conferred upon sick persons who requested it at least implicitly when they were in control of their faculties."[16] In short, if it can be presumed that the sick person would have requested the sacrament or at least would not have refused it, the priest may perform the rite. However, in cases where the sick person was known to have persisted in a manner of life contrary to the faith and did not, while conscious, manifest a change of heart, then Church law forbids conferral: "The anointing of the sick is not to be conferred upon those who obstinately persist in manifest serious sin."[17]

Anointing of the Sick is not a backdoor, last-minute vending machine by which someone who has persistently rejected their baptismal promises is admitted to heaven. If someone has purposefully lived a life in opposition to the faith and has not indicated a change of heart prior to facing death, the Church respects the life and identity that they have chosen for themselves and does not pretend on their behalf that they indicated otherwise. If someone has chosen not to identify themselves with the faith of their baptismal promises or openly rejected it, it would be as hypocritical for the Church to administer the sacrament to them as it would be for the person to accept it without a conversion of heart.

---

narios that priests are likely to find themselves in related to this point, see Keller, *The Sacraments of Healing*, 125.

[16] *The Code of Canon Law*, §1006.

[17] *The Code of Canon Law*, §1007.

The Church prays for the conversion of all sinners, but it is not for the Church or her ministers to redefine people's lives and choices for them in a way that is contrary to how they chose to live.

It is important to keep in mind that simply conferring a sacrament on someone (or encouraging them to receive a sacrament) does not guarantee that they will receive it fruitfully in the order of grace. In fact, on the contrary, encouraging someone to receive a sacrament who is not able to do so fruitfully can be a great disservice to them. Fr. Keller delicately explains this point: "For, to administer a sacrament, which presumes reconciliation with God and the Church, particularly at a time of serious illness, or even impending death, is to mislead a person into thinking that all is well when, in fact, it is not. The most merciful and pastoral act is to deal truthfully and honestly with the situation at hand."[18]

As I have written elsewhere, "the faithful could also be induced to presume that their external reception of the sacrament is fruitfully communicating its interior effects when, in fact, those effects would be impeded" by sin.[19] The same is also true for those who are encouraged to receive this sacrament without being in danger of death.

Children and the Mentally Disabled

In the Latin Church, *The Code of Canon Law* adds

---

[18] Keller, *The Sacraments of Healing*, 109.

[19] Roger W. Nutt, *General Principles of Sacramental Theology* (Washington D.C.: The Catholic University of America Press, 2017), 172.

that, in addition to beginning to be in the danger of death, eligible candidates of Anointing of the Sick must have also "reached the age of reason."[20] This means that the sacrament is normally not conferred upon children who have not received first Communion and Confession, as well as those with mental disabilities such that the partial exercise of reason is not possible. Parents of young children or children with mental disabilities who are facing death could understandably find this teaching of the Church to be especially challenging. It seems absurd that a baptized newborn struggling for its life or a two-year-old with Down syndrome facing major heart surgery would not be afforded the support of this sacrament. However, there is deep wisdom and insight in the Church's practice on this matter. Pastors need to be able to carefully explain this point to the faithful. Christ did not establish Anointing of the Sick so as to deprive those facing death from having to die. Rather, Christ gave the Church a sacrament for the sick so that they can die in union with him without being overcome in their weakened state by the bodily vulnerabilities and temptations that sinning can make us susceptible to.

Those who have not reached the age of reason cannot sin culpably. As a result, they are not in need of the grace that is conferred by this sacrament to prevent sinners from succumbing to sinful tendencies. This sacrament and Penance are categorized by the Church as healing sacraments— healing related to sin and its effects. The Church

---

[20] *The Code of Canon Law*, §1004.

does not withhold this sacrament from children or anyone else who might otherwise benefit from it. She withholds it from them because they are not in need of the specific form of healing that it has to offer. The "stuff" that this sacrament works on, the vulnerabilities that people have in a weakened state due to the remnants of sin, is not present in those who have not reached the age (or use) of reason.

The Code of Canon Law, however, as noted above, allows priests to make prudential judgments in particular cases. Children do not all reach the age of reason at the same moment. Not having reached the general age of first Communion is not an absolute indication that a particular child is incapable of using reason. When there is a question, the Church allows the priest to decide in favor of the sick person.

Distinguishing Penance and Anointing of the Sick: Eternal and Temporal Forgiveness

The fact that some "temporal consequences" of sin remain a part of the life of each follower of Christ even after Baptism helps explain why Christ instituted two sacraments ordered to post-baptismal healing. The Sacraments of Penance and Anointing of the Sick form a family of sacraments associated with healing in the Christian life: "The Lord Jesus Christ, physician of our souls and bodies, who forgave the sins of the paralytic and restored him to bodily health, has willed that his Church continue, in the power of the Holy Spirit, his work of healing and salvation, even among her own members.

This is the purpose of the two sacraments of healing: the sacrament of Penance and the sacrament of Anointing of the Sick."[21]

Sin wounds the bonds of union between the soul and God and the bonds that join believers to each other in Christ's Body. Mortal sin vitiates the union of charity uniting a soul to God *and* the Church. The grace of the sacrament of Penance heals and restores these lost bonds of unity between the sinner and God and the sinner and the members of Christ's Body. "The whole power of the sacrament of Penance consists in restoring us to God's grace and joining us with him in an intimate friendship," the *Catechism* teaches.

> Reconciliation with God is thus the purpose and effect of this sacrament. For those who receive the sacrament of Penance with contrite heart and religious disposition, reconciliation "is usually followed by peace and serenity of conscience with strong spiritual consolation." Indeed the sacrament of Reconciliation with God brings about a true "spiritual resurrection," restoration of the dignity and blessings of the life of the children of God, of which the most precious is friendship with God.[22]

Just as sin wounds our relationship with God and the members of the Church, so too is it the case that friendship with God unites us with God's friends:

---

[21] *CCC*, 1421.
[22] *CCC*, 1468.

"Sin damages or even breaks fraternal communion. The sacrament of Penance repairs or restores it. In this sense it does not simply heal the one restored to ecclesial communion, but has also a revitalizing effect on the life of the Church which suffered from the sin of one of her members."[23] As a result, the healing that is received in the Sacrament of Penance restores and revivifies the bonds of grace, especially charity, between God and neighbor that are wounded by our sins.

Why, then, is there need for another sacrament of healing besides Penance? Many of the observations above about the human condition converge on the answer to this question. Being forgiven by God through the graces of the Sacrament of Penance does not eliminate the remnants or temporal ramifications of sin in the life of the believer. As already noted, the struggle against sin and the tendency to sin remain after the forgiveness of Baptism and, subsequently, after Penance. Speaking of the distinction between the healing offered in Penance and Anointing of the Sick, Thomas Aquinas observes:

> Spiritual infirmities . . . are to be cured by penance, in that the works of virtue which the penitent performs when he makes satisfaction withdraw him from evils and incline him to good. But, since

---

[23] *CCC*, 1469. For a theological development of this point, see Giles Emery, O.P., "Reconciliation with the Church and Interior Penance: The Contribution of Thomas Aquinas on the Question of the *Res et Sacramentum* of Penance," *Nova et Vetera* 1, no. 2 (2003): 283–302.

man, whether due to negligence, or to the changing occupations of life, or even to the shortness of time, or to something else of the sort, does not perfectly heal within himself the weaknesses mentioned, a healthful provision for him is made by this sacrament: it completes the healing aforesaid, and it delivers him from the guilt of temporal punishment; as a result, nothing remains in him when the soul leaves the body which can obstruct the soul in perception of glory.[24]

A further, brief, exploration of the notion of remnants and temporal ramifications of sin is in order for the appreciation of this point. We most commonly tend to think of sin, whether original or personal, as a mark or stain on the soul that is wiped away by the graces received in the sacraments. Sin, however, is more than just a mark or stain that needs to be wiped away. Drawing on the resources of St. Thomas Aquinas's theology, Romanus Cessario offers the following explanation about the multifaceted nature of sin:

We call the "malum culpae" the stain of sin because it chiefly refers to the culpable alienation from God implied in the Christian notion of sin. Sin sullies the Christian soul. In addition, the metaphor of stain also points to the permanent character of

---

[24] Thomas Aquinas, *Summa contra gentiles*, book 4, *Salvation*, trans. Charles O'Neil (Notre Dame: University of Notre Dame Press, 1957), 283 (chapter 73).

sin or debt of punishment ("reatus poenae") which describes the abiding condition present in the sinner.[25]

The distinction between the "stain" of sin and the corresponding "abiding condition present in the sinner" is important for understanding the distinction between Penance and Anointing of the Sick. Baptism washes away all sin, original and personal. The graces of other sacraments, especially the Eucharist, can remit venial faults. The Sacrament of Penance remits both mortal and venial sin. However, as the distinction above clarifies, being forgiven of sins in Baptism or Penance cleanses the soul from the mark or stain but does not undo the remaining condition—weaknesses—caused by the fault. Because of the relationship between the soul and body, these remnants can afflict our bodily existence.

To illustrate this point with my students, I use the analogy of the child who throws a ball through a neighbor's window. If the neighbor forgives the child for the fault and sends them home forgiven and without penalty, the condition of the broken window remains even though forgiveness for the fault has been granted by the one offended. The forgiveness corresponds to and heals the stain or mark of the fault, but it does not undo all of the consequences or disorders caused by the fault—

---

[25] Romanus Cessario, OP, *The Godly Image: Christian Satisfaction in Aquinas* (Washington, D.C.: The Catholic University of America Press, 2020), 112–13. For a lengthier development of this point, see my *General Principles of Sacramental Theology*, 28ff.

the window remains broken even after the child who broke it has been forgiven. When we apply this to the human condition, we can see that just because we have obtained forgiveness for our sins in Baptism or later in Penance and other sacraments, it does not mean that the full impact of the consequences of those sins will not continue to plague us in the body throughout our temporal journey. Past sins, even when forgiven, can continue to tempt and pester us habitually, just like the lingering remnants of an old injury or a former addiction.

Following the teaching of Thomas Aquinas, who uses the analogy of the diverse medicines that are needed in relation to various conditions of bodily health, Romanus Cessario observes,

> One may be without illness but still not in good shape. Penance is ordered to spiritual health inasmuch as this sacrament brings healing from the illness of sin, whereas Holy Anointing restores robustness to a fatigued spiritual life. Its medicinal effects attend to the various remains of sin that weaken or limit a healthy but not vigorous spiritual life.[26]

Quitting a vice and receiving forgiveness for it does not mean that the effects of that vice will not linger and cause future vulnerabilities and temptations. The future effects of sins are often underappreciated. The short-term pleasures gained by sins in the

---

[26] Cessario, "Anointing of the Sick," 303.

present often scourge people disproportionately in the future. In his redemptive plan, God does not simply stop with forgiveness while leaving the disorders unaddressed. He actually fully restores to complete justice those whom he redeems.

Chapter IV

The Graces and Effects of Anointing of the Sick

Sacramental Grace Briefly Introduced

What makes the Sacrament of Anointing of the Sick such a profound gift to the Church is that the graces that it causes are ordered to assisting us when we are confronted by death due to sickness or old age. These graces help us overcome the vulnerabilities corresponding to the remnants of sin so the dying process can be accepted, spiritually fruitful, and made into an offering to God. The Council of Trent, in fact, recognizes the vulnerability that can accompany facing death as one of the reasons why the Lord instituted this sacrament:

> For though our adversary seeks and seizes opportunities through the whole of life of finding ways to devour our souls, yet there

is no time at which he draws more strongly
on every shred of skill to destroy us utterly,
and to deprive us, if he can, of our confidence in the divine mercy, than when
he sees that our departure from life is at
hand.[1]

It can be lost on Christians today how the gift
of grace impacts the soul and body from Baptism
throughout the believer's pilgrim journey toward
the attainment of eternal glory. Thomas Aquinas
identifies five effects of grace in the Christian life:
"The first is, to heal the soul; the second, to desire
good; the third, to carry into effect the good pro-
posed; the fourth, to persevere in good; the fifth,
to reach glory."[2] The sacraments are Christ's privileged way of sanctifying each Christian from the
healing of the soul to the ultimate attainment of
glory in heaven. Moreover, the grace caused by
each of the sacraments is not merely generic in
nature.

In addition to the healing, sanctification, and
elevation that is associated with the gift of grace
and the infused virtues and gifts, each sacrament
also provides graces that are necessary to support
Christians in the various stages of life and moments
of need. Thomas Aquinas explains the purpose of

---

[1] Council of Trent, in *Decrees of the Ecumenical Councils*, vol. 2,
Trent to Vatican II, ed. Norman P. Tanner, S.J. (Washington,
D.C.: Georgetown University Press, 1990), 711.

[2] Aquinas, *ST* I-II, q. 111, a. 3. Taken from Thomas Aquinas,
Summa theologiae, vol. 16, ed. John Mortensen and Enrique
Alarcón, trans. Laurence Shapcote, O.P. (Lander, WY: The
Aquinas Institute for the Study of Sacred Doctrine, 2012).

the sacraments vis-à-vis the unique graces that they cause for the sake of assisting Christians in various vocations and circumstances:

> Now the sacraments are ordained unto certain special effects which are necessary in the Christian life. . . . Consequently just as the virtues and gifts confer, in addition to grace commonly so called, a certain special perfection ordained to the powers' [of the soul] proper actions, *so does sacramental grace confer, over and above grace commonly so called, and in addition to the virtues and gifts, a certain Divine assistance in obtaining the end of the sacrament.*[3]

This important point is often misunderstood or hidden from non-Catholic Christians, especially those denominations that descend from the Reformation. Unfortunately, it has also even been somewhat deemphasized among Catholics. The Catholic and Orthodox Churches, which have maintained the seven sacraments that Christ instituted, recognize that Christ never meant for Baptism or the initial grace of salvation to be the sole moment of sanctification in the Christian life. The sacramental system of the Church provides important and needed graces to move and support the Christian

---

[3] Thomas Aquinas, *ST* III, q. 62, a. 2. Taken from Thomas Aquinas, *Summa theologiae*, vol. 20, ed. John Mortensen and Enrique Alarcon, trans. Laurence Shapcote, O.P. (Lander, WY: The Aquinas Institute for the Study of Sacred Doctrine, 2012), 24. Emphasis added.

from initial sanctification to eternal life.[4] Anointing of the Sick is not just another occasion for grace generically understood. As Paul Keller explains, "The ultimate aim of the sacrament [of Anointing of the Sick] is to usher us into the presence of God, preparing us for the beatific vision."[5] Like each of the sacraments that Christ instituted, Anointing of the Sick gives special graces that cluster around the strengthening, support, and forgiveness that are needed to assist the Christian in dying well so as to enter eternal glory. These graces join the Christian's weaknesses and act of dying to Christ's own suffering, making them spiritually efficacious.

The First Grace of Anointing

It is not easy to face death, especially in a weakened state. The wounds or remnants of sin that remain can make the dying person more susceptible to doubt, anger, fear, loneliness, despair, envy, and other vices that are harder to resist in a condition of physical weakness, exhaustion, and emotional fatigue. As a result, the *Catechism* teaches that the grace of this sacrament is

---

[4] For a helpful presentation of Thomas Aquinas's doctrine of deification, see Daria Spezzano, *The Glory of God's Grace: Deification according to St. Thomas Aquinas* (Ave Maria, FL: Sapientia Press of Ave Maria University, 2015).

[5] Paul Jerome Keller, O.P., *101 Questions & Answers on the Sacraments of Healing*: *Penance and Anointing of the Sick* (New York/Mahwah: Paulist Press, 2010), 102.

a particular gift of the Holy Spirit. The first grace of this sacrament is one of strengthening, peace and courage to overcome the difficulties that go with the condition of serious illness or the frailty of old age. This grace is a gift of the Holy Spirit, who renews trust and faith in God and strengthens against the temptations of the evil one, the temptation to discouragement and anguish in the face of death.[6]

It is important to note, contrary to the popular expectations of many Catholics, which can be fueled by the modern aversion to death and the bestowal of this sacrament to those who are not in danger of death, that the "first grace" of Anointing of the Sick is not physical healing. The object of this sacrament is not the evasion of death. This is one of the reasons why it was previously administered in closer conjunction to the moment of the death of the recipient. The *Catechism* reminds that "illness can lead to anguish, self-absorption, sometimes even despair and revolt against God."[7] The Church explains the gift of the Holy Spirit given in this sacrament in terms of strengthening against "difficulties" that accompany facing death. This grace of strengthening helps assist the recipient in trusting God and resisting temptations, such as discouragement, that can result from facing death in a weakened state.

It is natural, in a certain sense, for Catholics to

---

[6] *CCC*, 1520.

[7] *CCC*, 1501.

desire a miraculous healing for themselves or their loved ones. However, on the level of faith, we know that while death is the end of our earthly journey, it is not the end of human life itself. In fact, from the perspective of faith, we know that life with God in heaven is not only better than this life, but it is also our true purpose and destiny.

Christ does not redeem us from having to die; he redeems us from the condition of eternal loss— eternal separation from God after death. St. Paul ends his great teaching on the resurrection of the dead in 1 Corinthians 15:51–58 with the following words of encouragement:

> We shall not all sleep, but we shall all be changed, in a moment, in the twinkling of an eye, at the last trumpet. For the trumpet will sound, and the dead will be raised imperishable, and we shall be changed. For this perishable nature must put on the imperishable, and this mortal nature must put on immortality. When the perishable puts on the imperishable, and the mortal puts on immortality, then shall come to pass the saying that is written:
> "Death is swallowed up in victory."
> "O death, where is your victory?
> O death, where is your sting?"
> The sting of death is sin, and the power of sin is the law. But thanks be to God, who gives us the victory through our Lord Jesus Christ.
> Therefore, my beloved brethren, be stead-fast, immovable, always abounding in the

> work of the Lord, knowing that in the
> Lord your labor is not in vain.

Death in Christ is a passage from the perishable
to the imperishable. When joined to Christ, the
"labor" of living and dying is not in "vain." The
administration of Anointing of the Sick is an evangelical proclamation of Christ's victory over death
to those who are facing it. The reception of the
Sacrament of Anointing of the Sick more deeply
conforms the faithful to the risen Christ as they
pass from this life to eternity.

If a miraculous healing is granted by God
through this sacrament, which is very rare but
certainly possible, the miracle is not given to save
the healed person from death permanently. There
is a theological tradition in the Church that views
miraculous healing, if granted in conjunction with
this sacrament, as a gift given for the strengthening
of the faith of the sick person or their loved ones.
Even Lazarus, whom Jesus raised from the dead,
had to suffer death a second time to join Jesus in
heaven. When Jesus is first told of Lazarus's illness, he says that "it is for the glory of God, so that
the Son of God may be glorified by means of it"
(John 11:4). Then, when Lazarus dies, Jesus says,
"Lazarus is dead; and for your sake I am glad that
I was not there, so that you may believe. But let us
go to him" (John 11:14–15). Finally, just prior to
calling Lazarus forth from his tomb, Jesus states:
"Did I not tell you that if you would believe you
would see the glory of God?" (John 11:40). Jesus
consistently recommends his followers to have full
confidence in the power of his message instead of

seeking confirmation in signs and wonders. After Christ's resurrection, which Thomas said that he would not believe in without seeing the risen Christ, Jesus says to Thomas: "You have believed because you have seen me. Blessed are those who have not seen and yet believe" (John 20:29).

The visible healing is meant to manifest the invisible working of God, just as the visible anointing and words used to celebrate the sacrament signify the spiritual effects communicated by the sacrament. That is to say, in the words of Thomas Aquinas, any "outward" effect of the sacrament is given to signify and cause "spiritual healing."[8]

It is important for all of the faithful, and especially pastors and Catholic health care workers, to remind themselves and those who are ill of the actual theology of Anointing of the Sick and to encourage them to abandon themselves to God's will for their lives. If the primary expectation of the sick and their loved ones is for the avoidance of death by obtaining a miraculous cure, then they are fixed on a false hope that is not consistent with the message of the Gospel, and they are setting themselves up for disappointment. If a miraculous cure does not happen, it is not because the sacrament lacks power or efficacy, but because the "greater" miracle is the healing from the effects of sin so that we can die in union with Christ and enter into eternal glory. This truth should be a consolation, not a disappointment.

---

[8] Aquinas, *Commentary on the Sentences,* book IV, distinction 23, a. 2, questiuncula 2, trans. Beth Mortensen (Green Bay, WI: Aquinas Institute, Inc., 2017), 557.

Anointing for Death

The use of oil in the Old Testament and in the ancient world carries a more significant meaning than it does today. As a matter of fact, the significance of oil sheds further light on the purpose of this sacrament. In addition to the graces of strengthening, Anointing of the Sick also bestows "peace and courage . . . against the temptations of the evil one, the temptation to discouragement and anguish in the face of death."[9] By anointing the sick with oil while they are in danger of death, the Church consecrates them to God so that they can make their weakness, suffering, and death an offering to God.

The sacramental anointing that Christ commissioned the Church to bestow upon the sick joins their suffering with his. During his earthly journey, Christ touched every aspect of human life and the human condition: he lived in a family under the tutelage of Mary and Joseph; he blessed and received children in his company; he attended a wedding at Cana and spent time in the familial context of the home of Mary, Martha, and Lazarus; and he visited the sick, suffering, and marginalized. He also embraced a life of simplicity and poverty, of prayer and fasting, and suffered intense physical pain, public humiliation, betrayal, and death on a Cross.

The sacramental system of the Church continues Christ's presence in all of these spheres of human life. Just because Christ has ascended into heaven does not mean that he is no longer pres-

---

[9] *CCC*, 1520.

ent in the lives of believers from birth to death. Thomas Aquinas famously developed a theory of the seven sacraments that sees them corresponding on a spiritual plane to the way that biological life unfolds on the natural plane, culminating with the final healing needed for eternal glory:

> For spiritual life has a certain conformity with the life of the body: just as other corporeal things have a certain likeness to things spiritual. Now a man attains perfection in the corporeal life in two ways: first, in regard to his own person; secondly, in regard to the whole community of the society in which he lives, for man is by nature a social animal. With regard to himself man is perfected in the life of the body . . . by generation whereby a man begins to be and to live: and corresponding to this in the spiritual life there is Baptism, which is a spiritual regeneration, according to Titus 3:5: "By the laver of regeneration," etc. Secondly, by growth whereby a man is brought to perfect size and strength: and corresponding to this in the spiritual life there is Confirmation, in which the Holy Ghost is given to strengthen us. Wherefore the disciples who were already baptized were bidden thus: "Stay you in the city till you be endued with power from on high" (Luke 24:49). Thirdly, by nourishment, whereby life and strength are preserved to man; and corresponding to this in the spiritual life there is the Eucharist. Wherefore

it is said (John 6:54): "Except you eat of the flesh of the Son of Man, and drink His blood, you shall not have life in you."

And this would be enough for man if he had an impassible life, both corporally and spiritually; but since man is liable at times to both corporal and spiritual infirmity, i.e. sin, hence man needs a cure from his infirmity; which cure is twofold. One is the healing, that restores health: and corresponding to this in the spiritual life there is Penance, according to Psalm 40:5: "Heal my soul, for I have sinned against Thee." *The other is the restoration of former vigor by means of suitable diet and exercise: and corresponding to this in the spiritual life there is Extreme Unction, which removes the remainder of sin, and prepares man for final glory. Wherefore it is written (James 5:15): "And if he be in sins they shall be forgiven him."*[10]

Whether or not Thomas's analogy between spiritual and biological life works perfectly is not the central point. The point is that he recognizes that the sacramental system makes Christ's help and assistance available to his followers in every major phase of life and moment of need, from birth to death. When we read the Bible and see God's many amazing divine interventions into history, it can seem to us that God is now far away and distant. Aquinas's point, however, is that in the sacramental liturgy of the Church,

---

[10] Thomas Aquinas, *ST* III, q. 65, a. 1, p. 60. Emphasis added.

God continues to be actively present in history. Each sacrament is, in fact, a presence of God to us in the here and now. The anointing of Baptism and the anointing of Confirmation symbolize the spiritual consecration of the lives of each and every believer to participate in the Church's life of worship and to the public witness to the faith. The anointing of Holy Orders consecrates the ordained to a life of special ministry and service within the Church. Likewise, the Anointing of the Sick consecrates the recipient in their very condition of weakness to Christ's own suffering and passion.[11]

Even if one is already in the state of grace, the grace of each of the sacraments brings the presence of God to the believer in a newer and fuller way. The grace of Anointing of the Sick both gives the recipient added strength to persevere against temptations resulting from bodily weakness and joins the sick person to Christ's own suffering and weakness.

It can be tempting for those who are facing death to think that God is especially far away or has completely abandoned them. This sacrament mediates the close proximity that Christ has to the sick and dying in a unique and richly merciful fashion, and further deepens the union of the believer with Christ if they are already in the state of grace when the sacrament is received.

---

[11] For a helpful explanation of how the priestly ministry in the Sacrament of Anointing of the Sick "seals" the dying person in their illness and last moments to Christ, see J. Augustine DiNoia, O.P., and Joseph Fox, O.P., "Priestly Dimensions of the Sacrament of the Anointing of the Sick," *The Priest* 62 (2006): 10–13.

The Grace of Suffering with Christ

Christ's incarnation turned the tragedy of the Fall, and the power of the "Prince of this world," on its head. In light of Christ's life and teaching, suffering and death have taken on a new meaning and significance. In his encyclical on the "saving" meaning of suffering, St. John Paul II notes a certain joy that can accompany suffering as a result of embracing it in union with Christ:

> Saint Paul speaks of such joy in the Letter to the Colossians: "I rejoice in my sufferings for your sake." A source of joy is found in the *overcoming of the sense of the uselessness of suffering,* a feeling that is sometimes very strongly rooted in human suffering. This feeling not only consumes the person interiorly, but seems to make him a burden to others. The person feels condemned to receive help and assistance from others, and at the same time seems useless to himself. The discovery of the salvific meaning of suffering in union with Christ *transforms* this depressing *feeling.*[12]

Those who are united to Christ can join their suffering to his, thus giving it a spiritual dimension. While in a certain sense Christ has solidarity with all who suffer, Anointing of the Sick confers a spe-

---

[12] St. John Paul II, *Salvifici Doloris* (February 11, 1984), §27, http://www.vatican.va/content/john-paul-ii/en/apost_letters/1984/documents/hf_jp-ii_apl_11021984_salvifici-doloris.html.

cial conformity in grace of the recipient of the sacrament to Christ:

> By the grace of this sacrament the sick person receives the strength and the gift of uniting himself more closely to Christ's Passion: in a certain way he is consecrated to bear fruit by configuration to the Savior's redemptive Passion. Suffering, a consequence of original sin, acquires a new meaning; it becomes a participation in the saving work of Jesus.[13]

Because Anointing of the Sick joins those approaching death to Christ's passion through the particular effect of the sacrament, their suffering takes on an added dimension that makes it an instrument of Christ's work of redemption. When accepted under the light of the Christian faith, the union with Christ caused by the Sacrament of Anointing of the Sick makes the sick person's very weakness and proximity to death a source of prayer and spiritual offering. Far from being pointless and without meaning, when joined to Christ sacramentally, the acceptance of suffering and the act of dying itself can be offered to God as extensions of Christ's own redemptive work. "Faith in sharing in the suffering of Christ," St. John Paul II explains,

> brings with it the interior certainty that the suffering person "completes what is lacking in Christ's afflictions"; the certainty that

---

[13] *CCC*, 1521.

in the spiritual dimension of the work of Redemption *he is serving*, like Christ, *the salvation of his brothers and sisters.* Therefore he is carrying out an irreplaceable service. In the Body of Christ, which is ceaselessly born of the Cross of the Redeemer, it is precisely suffering permeated by the spirit of Christ's sacrifice that *is the irreplaceable mediator and author of the good things* which are indispensable for the world's salvation. It is suffering, more than anything else, which clears the way for the grace which transforms human souls. Suffering, more than anything else, makes present in the history of humanity the powers of the Redemption. In that "cosmic" struggle between the spiritual powers of good and evil . . . human sufferings, united to the redemptive suffering of Christ, *constitute a special support for the powers of good,* and open the way to the victory of these salvific powers.[14]

What John Paul II indicates in this remarkable passage is that, when coupling their suffering with the power of Christ's own suffering, those in a state of physical weakness or near death can be a great source of grace and redemption for the world. Their acceptance of suffering in union with Christ is a "service" that the sick and dying can offer to God for the benefit of themselves and others. As a result, the redemptive value of suffering, when

---

[14] St. John Paul II, *Salvifici Doloris*, §27.

it is joined to Christ, can benefit and enrich the Church, just as the sick person is strengthened by Christ through the sacrament.

In fact, there is a reciprocal relationship between the sick person's reliance on the Church for the graces of the sacrament and the Church's reliance on the sick person for her growth in holiness. "The sick who receive this sacrament," the *Catechism* teaches,

> "by freely uniting themselves to the passion and death of Christ," "contribute to the good of the People of God." By celebrating this sacrament the Church, in the communion of saints, intercedes for the benefit of the sick person, and he, for his part, though the grace of this sacrament, contributes to the sanctification of the Church and to the good of all men for whom the Church suffers and offers herself through Christ to God the Father.[15]

Even though people who are approaching death because of sickness or old age are, from a physical standpoint, quite powerless, it is most certainly not the case that they have nothing to offer the Church or God. Their very weakness, when accepted in faith and joined to Christ, is a source and instrument of spiritual growth and opportunities for themselves and others. In the same way, therefore, that we speak of a "baptismal," "Eucharistic," or "priestly" spirituality, Anointing of the Sick

---

[15] *CCC*, 1522.

opens the way for a spirituality of suffering and dying. "The anointed Christian," Colman O'Neill explains, "offering himself as a victim, accepting his own suffering and death in conformity with Christ, can find in them a new baptism from which he will rise up, as Christ did, to glory."[16]

In fact, Fr. Jean-Philippe Revel points out that it is through their acceptance of suffering and their conformity to Christ that the dying participate in the common baptismal priesthood. By being conformed to Christ's own suffering, those who receive Anointing of the Sick assume an important role and office within the Christian community.[17] Those who reject suffering as pointless and seek to euthanize or assist the sick in taking their own lives are cheating them of one of the richest and most meaningful phases of the human journey. As St. John Paul II teaches in his encyclical letter, *The Gospel of Life*,

> what might seem logical and humane, when looked at more closely is seen to be senseless and inhumane. Here we are faced

---

[16] O'Neill, Colman E. O'Neill, *Meeting Christ in the Sacraments* (New York: Alba House, 1991), 292. O'Neill adds to this point: "Here, then, is the function of anointing as a sacrament of the sick. It enables the Christian to incorporate ill-health into the life of the Church. For not only does it make suffering meaningful and profitable for the individual; through his acceptance of pain, the Church takes on more vividly the characteristics of Christ and is made more perfect as his sacrament in the world" (289).

[17] Jean-Philippe Revel, *Traité des sacrements*, vol. 6, *L'onction des maladies: Rédemption de la chair par la chair* (Paris: Éditions du Cerf, 2009), 189.

with one of the more alarming symptoms of the "culture of death," which is advancing above all in prosperous societies, marked by an attitude of excessive preoccupation with efficiency and which sees the growing number of elderly and disabled people as intolerable and too burdensome. These people are very often isolated by their families and by society, which are organized almost exclusively on the basis of criteria of productive efficiency, according to which a hopelessly impaired life no longer has any value.[18]

Suffering and weakness might be useless to those who worship brute force and physical productivity, but as the life of Christ teaches, the condition of weakness and vulnerability is God's chosen vessel for manifesting his true power. The suffering and dying must also follow the pattern highlighted at the foot of the Cross and turn their ordeals over to Mary's maternal role in the life of the Church. "As a mother," John Paul II teaches,

[Mary] also wishes the messianic power of her Son to be manifested, that salvific power of his which is meant to help man in his misfortunes, to free him from the evil which in various forms and degrees weighs heavily upon his life. Precisely as the Prophet Isaiah had foretold about the Messiah in the famous

---

[18] St. John Paul II, *Evangelium Vitae* (March 25, 1995), §64.3, http://www.vatican.va/content/john-paul-ii/en/encyclicals/documents/hf_jp-ii_enc_25031995_evangelium-vitae.html.

passage which Jesus quoted before his fellow townsfolk in Nazareth: "To preach good news to the poor . . . to proclaim release to the captives and recovering of sight to the blind . . ." (cf. Lk. 4:18).[19]

Anointing of the Sick provides the healing that the sick and suffering need to make their ordeal fruitful. "While bodily illness may be an occasion of spiritual good," John Boyle explains, "as a form of satisfaction for sins . . . such illness may also impede spiritual health as when the weakness of the body impedes the exercise of the virtues. Because therefore the body ought to be properly disposed to the soul, it is only fitting that there be a spiritual medicine directed to corporeal illness as it arises from sin."[20] In fact, Anointing of the Sick strengthens the ability to suffer and die virtuously for Christ.[21]

---

[19] St. John Paul II, *Redemptoris Mater: On the Blessed Virgin Mary in the Life of the Pilgrim Church* (March 25, 1987), §21, http://www.vatican.va/content/john-paul-ii/en/encyclicals/documents/hf_jp-ii_enc_25031987_redemptoris-mater.html.

[20] John Boyle, "Saint Thomas Aquinas on the Anointing of the Sick," in *Rediscovering Aquinas and the Sacraments*, ed. Michael Dauphinais and Matthew Levering (Chicago: Hillenbrand Books, 2009), 80.

[21] In the so-called "supplementum" to the third part of his *Summa theologiae*, which was compiled by Aquinas's students after his death, the "*res et sacramentum*" or immediate effect of the sacrament is identified as a "certain interior devotion" (*quaedam interior devotio*). This understanding, while perhaps underdeveloped, does intimate a clear understanding of the spiritual or interior graces to die virtuously—to die devotedly—that Anointing of the Sick causes in the recipient. See *ST supplementum*, q. 30, a. 3, ad 3, found in Thomas Aquinas, *Summa Theo-*

It is difficult for the faithful, especially because of the remnants of sin, to accept suffering and to surrender themselves to God's will. "When, with the help of the sacrament," Matthew Levering explains, "dying persons are freed of all impediments to surrendering themselves to God, they discover, in Andrew Davidson's words, 'what it means to share in Christ'—and thus in his dying—'*right to the end.*'"[22] Far from being without meaning, making of one's death an offering to God through Christ is a most courageous and fruitful end to an earthly pilgrimage. For St. Paul this truth was a cornerstone of discipleship: "For the sake of Christ, then, I am content with weaknesses, insults, hardships, persecutions, and calamities; for when I am weak, then I am strong" (2 Cor 12:10).

Anointing, Viaticum, and the Grace to Transition from Time to Eternity

Because death is not the cessation of life for human beings but is instead the end of our earthly journey, the graces of the Sacrament of Anointing of the Sick enable us to cling to God as our time in this life passes from us. The attitude toward death found in the earliest Christians helps us to see how far contemporary attitudes toward death have wandered from the foundations of the faith.

---

logica, vol. 5, trans. Fathers of the English Dominican Province (New York, NY: Benzinger Bros., 1948), 2661.

[22] Levering, *Dying and the Virtues* (Grand Rapids, MI: William B. Eerdmans Publishing Company, 2018), 145.

St. Paul's mindset about life and death is hardly believable today for those who can scarcely even think of death: "For to me to live is Christ, and to die is gain. If it is to be life in the flesh, that means fruitful labor for me. Yet which I shall choose I cannot tell. I am hard pressed between the two. My desire is to depart and be with Christ, for that is far better. But to remain in the flesh is more necessary on your account" (Phil 1:21–24). Paul's view that "to die is gain" and his desire to "depart and be with Christ" is rooted in his firm knowledge of eternal life as a result of Christ's victory over death.

This attitude is not just unique to St. Paul. St. Ignatius of Antioch, who died a martyr around AD 107, wrote the following while in the custody of Roman soldiers en route to his execution in Rome. In this passage, Ignatius begs the Christians of Rome to not intervene on his behalf because he understands his earthly life to be death and life in heaven to be the true fullness of life:

> All the pleasures of the world, and all the kingdoms of this earth, shall profit me nothing. It is better for me to die on behalf of Jesus Christ, than to reign over all the ends of the earth. For what shall a man be profited, if he gain the whole world, but lose his own soul? Him I seek, who died for us: Him I desire, who rose again for our sake. This is the gain which is laid up for me. Pardon me, brethren: do not hinder me from living, do not wish to keep me in a state of death; and while I desire to belong to God, do not give me over to the world.

Allow me to obtain pure light: when I have gone there, I shall indeed be a man of God. Permit me to be an imitator of the passion of my God. If any one has Him within himself, let him consider what I desire, and let him have sympathy with me, as knowing how I am straitened.[23]

This attitude of St. Ignatius of Antioch is no doubt heroic and the result of a singular grace. The Church does not expect each and every Christian to be so bold in the face of death and suffering; the Church does not expect every Christian to hasten toward blood-martyrdom in this way. Yet, from the example of Christ himself, as well as those of St. Paul, St. Ignatius, and so many other saints and martyrs, Christians today can learn that death should not be viewed as the end or even as a defeat. Because of Christ's victory over death, the Christian can view the end of life in a fundamentally unique way among world religions and systems of thought.

The Church teaches that death can be viewed by each follower of Christ as a special calling from God: "In death, God calls man to himself. Therefore the Christian can experience a desire for death like St. Paul's: 'My desire is to depart and be with Christ.' He can transform his own death into an act of obedience and love towards the Father, after

---

[23] St. Ignatius of Antioch, "The Epistle of Ignatius to the Romans," trans. Alexander Roberts and James Donaldson, in *Ante-Nicene Fathers*, vol. 1, ed. Alexander Roberts, James Donaldson, and A. Cleveland Coxe (Buffalo, NY: Christian Literature Publishing Co., 1885), 12, https://www.newadvent.org/fathers/0107.htm.

the example of Christ."[24] At death, therefore, God calls each person to be with him.

It is important to note that the ending of one's temporal journey is revealed to be definitive.[25] Because of this truth, it is extremely healthy from a spiritual standpoint to reflect upon death and mortality. We do not all know the moment of our death, but we most certainly know that we shall all die. Some internalization of this fact and preparation for it is not only healthy but prudent. Whether it is in internal conversation with ourselves or in giving care to others, honesty about our own or someone else's condition is a true act of charity. By reflecting on our mortality, we can avoid being spiritually blindsided if serious illness or injury comes upon us quickly. A basic but forgotten tenet of Christian spirituality is the call to unceasing vigilance in light of the fact that the moment of our death and the time of the Lord's coming are unknown: "Watch therefore, for you know neither

---

[24] *CCC*, 1011.

[25] This point is a basic tenet of the Christian faith: the afterlife is not a cycle of reincarnation; death ends the journey, and judgment follows death. That is to say, whenever a person's earthly life is ended, there is no other temporal phase by which he may change his eternal destiny. For many very good reasons, both philosophical and theological, Christianity rejects cyclical views of eternal life in which one may "try again" after death. "Death is the end of man's earthly pilgrimage," the *Catechism* teaches, "of the time of grace and mercy which God offers him so as to work out his earthly life in keeping with the divine plan, and to decide his ultimate destiny. When 'the single course of our earthly life' is completed, we shall not return to other earthly lives: 'It is appointed for men to die once.' There is no 'reincarnation' after death" (*CCC*, 1013).

the day nor the hour" (Matt 25:13).

One of the additional graces of the Sacrament of Anointing of the Sick is that it prepares those in danger of death for the final stage of the journey to their heavenly homeland. "If the sacrament of anointing of the sick is given to all who suffer from serious illness and infirmity," the *Catechism* explains, "even more rightly is it given to those at the point of departing this life; so it is also called *sacramentum exeuntium* (the sacrament of those departing)."[26] It is not only a sacrament for the sick solely because they are dying; it is also a sacrament for them because in death they pass from this life to the next. Because death is not the end of one's existence, but the entrance into a new and final stage of life—eternal life—Christ uses this sacrament to assist the dying in safely passing from this life to the next. It is this sacrament that gives the dying the final conformity to Christ that is needed to freely pass from this life to the life of eternal glory.

The supernatural life that is begun with the graces of Baptism and augmented with the other sacraments is brought to completion with this last sacrament: "The Anointing of the Sick completes our conformity to the death and Resurrection of Christ, just as Baptism began it. It completes the holy anointings that mark the whole Christian life: that of Baptism which sealed the new life in us, and that of Confirmation which strengthened us for the combat of this life. This last anointing fortifies the end of our earthly life like a solid rampart for the final struggles before entering the Father's

---

[26] *CCC*, 1523.

house."[27] Therefore, Christ does not intend the Christian life of grace to be sustained solely by the graces of Christian initiation or the sacraments received throughout one's life, including Penance. The manifold graces of Anointing of the Sick are intended by Christ to bring the whole life of grace to completion and eternal rest.

In conjunction with receiving the final anointings of our earthly journey, which especially fortifies the soul and joins the recipient to Christ, the reception of Holy Communion is made uniquely fruitful. "In addition to the Anointing of the Sick," the *Catechism* notes,

> the Church offers those who are about to leave this life the Eucharist as viaticum. Communion in the body and blood of Christ, received at this moment of "passing over" to the Father, has a particular significance and importance. It is the seed of eternal life and the power of resurrection, according to the words of the Lord: "He who eats my flesh and drinks my blood has eternal life, and I will raise him up at the last day." The sacrament of Christ once dead and now risen, the Eucharist is here the sacrament of passing over from death to life, from this world to the Father.[28]

Anointing of the Sick, which gives those facing death unique graces to persevere to the end in

---

[27] *CCC*, 1523.
[28] *CCC*, 1524.

union with Christ, is fittingly complemented by the fruitful reception of the Eucharist. In John 6:54, Christ promised that the Eucharist would cause eternal life and resurrection of the body in those who receive it. As a result, there is a deep spiritual benefit to passing from this life under the assistance of the two sacraments of healing, Penance and Anointing of the Sick, fortified by the Eucharist.

The Church teaches that just as Baptism, Confirmation, and the Eucharist form an initial grouping as the sacraments of initiation, "Penance, the Anointing of the Sick and the Eucharist as viaticum constitute at the end of Christian life 'the sacraments that prepare for our heavenly homeland' or the sacraments that complete the earthly pilgrimage."[29] The connection of Anointing of the Sick with Communion given as Viaticum further indicates the relation of this sacrament to death. Indeed, if Anointing of the Sick were not ordered to assisting those facing death, then the practice of coupling it with Communion—spiritual food for the journey—for those passing from this life would not make sense. "The Eucharist of course," Matthew Levering explains, "does not bring us immediately into eternal life. The Eucharist is called 'viaticum,' food for the journey, because it 'does not once admit us to glory, but bestows on us the power of coming unto glory.'"[30]

---

[29] *CCC*, 1525.

[30] Matthew Levering, *Jesus and the Demise of Death: Resurrection, Afterlife, and the Fate of the Christian* (Waco, TX: Baylor University Press, 2012), 75. The citation in this quotation is from Aquinas's *Summa theologiae*, III, q. 79, a. 2, ad 1.

When supported by the full richness of the sacramental life, those who face death are surrounded by the presence of Christ, who is there for them through the ministry of the Church, by the mediation of these three sacraments (Penance, Anointing, and Viaticum). Far from being abandoned or alone in this time of weakness, the sick person is supported according to their deepest spiritual needs by Anointing of the Sick and the other sacraments that they are able to receive. Just as the blood of the sacrificed lambs sprinkled on the doorposts of the Jewish people in Egypt saved their firstborn from death on the night of the first Passover (see Exod 12), so too do the sacraments save each Christian when they pass from this life to the next.

The Grace of Forgiveness of Sins

The Church teaches that another grace of Anointing of the Sick is the forgiveness of sins. The passage in James 5 that promulgates the celebration of the sacrament also affirms that if the recipient "has committed sins, he will be forgiven" (v. 15). There are many converging theological reasons why God has ordained that sins be forgiven in this sacrament. First, as a sacrament of healing, Anointing of the Sick maintains an organic relationship with the Sacrament of Penance. In fact, in its teaching against the reformers, the Council of Trent introduces its chapters on the Anointing of the Sick by indicating that it seemed to them good to "add" to the teaching on Penance. Anointing of the Sick, the Tridentine fathers explain, "was considered by the Fathers as the consummation not only of penance but also of the whole Christian life, which ought to be a continual penance."[31]

So Anointing of the Sick consummates the penitential life of the faithful by conferring "the grace of the Holy Spirit, whose anointing takes away the sins, if there be any to be expiated, and also the remains of sin."[32] This teaching is fundamentally consoling, but it ought not to lead the faithful to presumption. Anointing of the Sick is not, as noted above, a vending machine for forgiveness. It is, along with Penance, a sacrament of healing. Christ heals from sin by calling the faithful to conversion. Anointing of the Sick, therefore, does not heal from sin souls who have not sought, in any way, to live lives of conversion and penitence.

In the Sacrament of Penance, the faithful bring three principles that are necessary for the efficacy of the sacrament: (1) the confession of their sins; (2) sorrow or contrition for the sins they are confessing; and (3) a genuine resolution of the heart to change that is manifest in the acceptance and performance of the penance that is assigned by the priest. If a penitent consciously fails to confess mortal sins to the priest, is not truly sorry for the sins he has committed and confessed, or is not willing to do penance for his wrongdoing, he does

---

[31] Council of Trent, Session 14, November 25, 1551. Henrich Denzinger, *Compendium of Creeds, Definitions, and Declarations on Matters of Faith and Morals*, 43rd ed., ed. Peter Hünermann (San Francisco: Ignatius Press, 2012), 408 (§1694).

[32] Council of Trent, Session 14. In Denzinger, *Compendium of Creeds, Definitions, and Declarations*, 409 (§1696).

not bring what is needed on his part to make the Sacrament of Penance work efficaciously. The forgiveness that is bestowed in Anointing of the Sick is likewise dependent upon the disposition of the recipient: Anointing of the Sick cannot complete or consummate Penance if there is nothing to be completed or consummated.

This is already hinted at in the Church's canonical practice of withholding the sacrament from "those who obstinately persist in manifest serious sin."[33] Just how Holy Anointing effects the forgiveness of sin is a matter on which theologians have disagreed. It is beyond the aim of this volume to adjudicate this question with precision. However, it seems safe to indicate that the scope of forgiveness and fruitfulness that are bestowed in this sacrament are likely to be related to the disposition of the recipient especially in relation to their contrition for sins.[34] For example, if someone who cultivated an interior life and went to Confession as needed or according to a regular schedule and suddenly fell ill and into an unconscious state without being able to confess, it seems likely that their favorable disposition to Penance would be amenable to the graces of forgiveness. If, however, someone rejected the importance of the Sacrament

---

[33] *The Code of Canon Law (1983)*, §1007, https://www.vatican.va/archive/cod-iuris-canonici/cic_index_en.html.

[34] Colman O'Neill takes this position: "Should the recipient be in a state of grave sin, and granted that he has such sorrow as is compatible with this state—that is, attrition—anointing will bring him absolution. The normal case envisaged here is that of an unconscious Catholic and it is in this situation that anointing enjoys a decided advantage over penance" (O'Neill, *Meeting Christ in the Sacraments*, 287).

of Penance, even when needed, and likewise had no thought or intention of changing course, and this person were to suddenly fall ill and unconscious, it seems unlikely that the sacrament would find a disposition in the recipient that is conducive to forgiveness. It is worth quoting Thomas Aquinas at length on the relation between the remissions of sin and the conferral of grace by this sacrament:

> [Anointing of the Sick is] against those defects by which a person is spiritually ill and does not have the complete strength for acts of grace and glory. And this defect is nothing other than a certain weakness and unsuitability that is left in us from actual or original sin; and against this weakness a person is strengthened by this sacrament. But because grace causes this strength, which is not compatible with sin, therefore as a result if it encounters any sin, whether mortal or venial in guilt, it takes it away, as long as no obstacle is placed on the part of the recipient. . . . For it does not always blot out sin, since it does not always find it, but it always remits as to the weakness mentioned, which some people call the remains of sin. . . .
>
> Therefore, it should be said that the chief effect of this sacrament is the remission of sins as to the traces left by sin; but as to guilt, if it encounters it, as a result.[35]

---

[35] Thomas Aquinas, *Commentary on the Sentences*, book IV, distinction 23, a. 2, response to questiuncula 1, trans. Beth Mortensen (Green Bay, WI: Aquinas Institute, Inc., 2017), 558.

The Church has long resisted seating the objective causal power of the sacraments in the fervor of the faith of the minister or the recipients. The *ex opere operato* doctrine clarifies that Christ, not the faithful, is the principal agent in the sacraments. However, the Church has also clearly affirmed that the fruitfulness of the reception of validly celebrated sacraments is impacted by the disposition of the recipients. Thus, the fact that the Church teaches that sin can be forgiven by the sacrament of the sick does not mean that the requisite disposition to be forgiven is possessed by everyone who happens to receive the sacrament.

Chapter V

Toward a Theology of Rites and the Rite of Anointing of the Sick

A Sacramental Theology of Rites

The rite that the Church has promulgated for the celebration of Anointing of the Sick reveals many of the theological truths intrinsic to the sacrament. The understanding and expectations that the faithful have about Anointing of the Sick should be informed by what the sacrament discloses about itself. It is important to keep in mind that while the Church uses many different signs and symbols in her worship, including holy water, incense, icons, and various actions and gestures, the seven sacraments of the Church are privileged and unique. In communities and civil society, the meaning of some signs and symbols is dictated solely by convention. For example, a red octagonal sign with the letters *STOP* on it conveys to drivers that they must stop their vehicles.

With these types of signs and symbols there is not a natural and internal correspondence between the symbol and the act of stopping. Stop signs could just as easily be blue and rectangular. The connection between the sign and the act of stopping is made by the conventions of the community.

The symbols used by the Church in the celebration of the sacraments are not arbitrary in the way that (strictly) conventional signs are. When the Church uses symbols and signs in her worship, these symbols and signs have a connection to the reality that they signify or symbolize. This connection comes from the author of each sacrament, who is none other than Jesus Christ. In the same way that the words of Scripture unveil revealed truth to the human mind, so too do the words and signs used in the sacraments unveil the hidden spiritual realities given by the rite. In this way, the celebration of Anointing of the Sick should be viewed as a proclamation of the Gospel to the recipient and their loved ones—the rite unveils God's ongoing saving activity through the Church.

What makes the sacraments unique is that they actually cause the spiritual effects that are intrinsic to what they signify or symbolize. This is not the case with other sacramentals and symbols used by the Church. Water naturally symbolizes cleansing and hydration, and the Church teaches that Baptism washes the soul clean from sin and infuses into it the new life of grace. Baptism does not cleanse and vivify the soul by grace simply because of the natural signification of water as a source of hydration and cleansing. The history of salvation clarifies the meaning and use of water in the plan of God.

From the Flood, the Red Sea, and the crossing of the Jordan to enter the Holy Land, to John's baptism, Jesus's own reception of baptism, and Jesus's institution of Baptism, the use of water in the Church's worship carries with it all of these additional, divinely inspired meanings. In the same way that the Israelites were delivered from their pursuers by God's parting of the Red Sea, Christians are likewise delivered from sin by the administration of Baptism. The same could be said for all of the sacraments. Each of them has been appropriated by God and instituted by Christ for special use within the Church's worship that is ordered to the conferral of spiritual effects on the soul in the form of sacramental grace and—in the case of Baptism, Confirmation, and Holy Orders—sacramental character.

The meaning of the sacramental rites, therefore, is not merely "horizontal" like the meaning of a stop sign. The material sign or symbol of every sacrament is also informed by the words used in the rite. Washing or pouring water over someone does not confer Baptism. Rather, Baptism is performed when the application of water upon someone's head (or their submersion in it) is coupled with the form given by Christ in Matthew 28:19 to baptize "in the name of the Father and of the Son and of the Holy Spirit." The sign of a material element and the words of the rite (celebrated by the proper minister with the requisite intention) together constitute the sacrament by which the spiritual effect is caused and conferred upon the recipient by Christ.

The primary meaning of each sacrament, therefore, is derived from Christ's authority as God in instituting each sacrament as a particular form of worship ordered to particular needs in the Christian moral and spiritual life. Thomas Aquinas, for example, clarifies that the spiritual power of the sacraments is established and sustained by the power and authority of God, who gave the Church the sacraments for the sake of using them to confer these spiritual effects: "He who institutes the sacraments," Aquinas clarifies, is distinguishable from

> he who makes use of the sacrament instituted, by applying it for the production of the effect. Now the power of a sacrament cannot be from him who makes use of the sacrament: because he works but as a minister. Consequently, it follows that the power of the sacrament is from the institutor of the sacrament. Since, therefore, the power of the sacrament is from God alone, it follows that God alone can institute the sacraments.[1]

This is why the Church does not allow alteration of the matter or words of a sacrament: the spiritual effect is contained in the sign. If the sign is altered or frustrated by a manipulation of the words or matter, it may no longer be the sign that Christ instituted for the conferral of this particular effect of grace. Motor oil, for example, does not symbolize cleansing and therefore cannot be used as a substitute for water in the celebration

---

[1] Thomas Aquinas, *ST* III, q. 64, a. 2, p. 45. Taken from *Summa theologiae*, vol. 20, ed. John Mortensen and Enrique Alarcon, trans. Laurence Shapcote, O.P. (Lander, WY: The Aquinas Institute for the Study of Sacred Doctrine, 2012), 45.

of Baptism. Likewise, even a cleaning agent like bleach is not valid for use in the Sacrament of Baptism because bleach was not an instrument used by God throughout the salvation history to bring about cleansing and liberation, nor was it indicated by Christ as valid matter when he instituted the sacrament.

Each sacramental sign, therefore, participates in some way in the sanctifying reality that it symbolizes. This is why appreciating the significance of the matter and form used in each rite is helpful in understanding the effects conferred by each sacrament. Unlike the stop sign, whose meaning is arbitrary and wholly extrinsic to the act of stopping, the sacraments, as divinely established signs, actually share in and bring about the spiritual reality that they signify. From a liturgical standpoint, when a priest (or bishop) celebrates the sacrament of the sick by anointing a sick member of the faithful with oil and saying the appropriate prayers, the sign that is brought about confers upon the recipient the graces signified by the sign.

The seven sacraments did not emanate from the early Church or the life of ancient Israel solely as cultural artifacts. While the sacraments do bear the mark of the Judeo-Christian culture of the ancient Near East, their primary meaning comes from their place in the providential plan of God and from Christ's intention for the order of the Church's life of worship. As noted above, the ministry to the sick was integral both to Christ's own public ministry and to the ministry that he transmitted to the Apostles.

As a result, Christ instituted the Sacrament of

Anointing of the Sick to signify his ongoing presence and ministry to the sick through his priest, and, through this sacrament, he confers the effects symbolized by the sign on those who receive it. The Church articulates this point through her doctrine of sacramental causality:

> This is the meaning of the Church's affirmation that the sacraments act *ex opere operato* (literally: "by the very fact of the action's being performed"), i.e., by virtue of the saving work of Christ, accomplished once for all. It follows that "the sacrament is not wrought by the righteousness of either the celebrant or the recipient, but by the power of God." From the moment that a sacrament is celebrated in accordance with the intention of the Church, the power of Christ and his Spirit acts in and through it, independently of the personal holiness of the minister.[2]

So the Church's ministry to the sick through this sacrament is not a hollow symbol but a secure and certain source of the graces that Christ imbued this rite with when he instituted it. Every valid sacramental celebration, since it does not depend on the worthiness of the minister or recipient for its objective power, indicates an efficacious work of Christ and the Holy Spirit.

Because the spiritual effects of each sacrament are intrinsic to the motion of the rites when prop-

---

[2]   *CCC*, 1128.

erly celebrated, and not the holiness of the minister or the recipient, the sacraments have a unique and privileged standing in the Church's spirituality and life of prayer. In fact, Christ more closely associates himself with the sacramental acts of the Church than any other Christian activity: "To accomplish so great a work, Christ is always present in His Church, especially in her liturgical celebrations. . . . By His power He is present in the sacraments, so that when a man baptizes it is really Christ Himself who baptizes."[3] The operative power of Christ's priestly presence in each of the sacramental rites leads the Church to the following conclusion: "From this it follows that every liturgical celebration, because it is an action of Christ the priest and of His Body which is the Church, is a sacred action surpassing all others; no other action of the Church can equal its efficacy by the same title and to the same degree."[4]

As a result, every sacramental rite of the Church must be understood in light of this theological foundation. When someone validly receives the Sacrament of Anointing of the Sick, the sacramental rite is a work of Christ himself conferring the gift of the Spirit in the form of grace. The objective efficacy of each sacrament cannot be exceeded by any other spiritual activity of the Church. This is why the celebration of Anointing of the Sick, and each of the sacraments, should be viewed as a proc-

---

[3] Second Vatican Council, *Sacrosanctum Concilium*, in *Decrees of the Ecumenical Councils*, vol. 2, *Trent to Vatican II*, ed. Norman P. Tanner, S.J. (Washington, D.C.: Georgetown University Press, 1990), §7.1.

[4] Vatican II, *Sacrosanctum Concilium*, §7.4.

lamation of the Gospel. In the celebration of each sacrament, God's saving plan of salvation in Christ is brought to fruition, if the sacrament is validly celebrated and worthily received.

The Rite of Anointing of the Sick

With this theological context in mind, we can now examine the rite of Anointing of the Sick.[5] With each sacrament the Church identifies an "essential rite" that constitutes the core component of the celebration. With Baptism, for example, the essential rite is the application of water (to an unbaptized recipient) and the invocation of the Trinitarian formula by a minister with the requisite intention. Baptism can—and should—be celebrated with the fuller rite, if possible, as is the case with Baptisms celebrated during the Easter Vigil, in the context of the Eucharistic liturgy. The same is true for many other sacraments, including Anointing of the Sick.

The distinction between the essential rite of each sacrament and the broader celebration that often surrounds the essential rite is explained by Thomas Aquinas in terms of the reverence and devotion that ought to accompany each sacra-

---

[5] Theologians and Christian historians today often subordinate the theology of the sacraments to a consideration of the rites. The proper order, however, is to understand the rite in light of the theology of the sacrament. The rites emerged from Christ's institution of each sacrament, not vice versa. The Church would not have a sacramental liturgy and various rites if Christ had not given the Church sacramental acts of worship.

ment. The Church does not arbitrarily "make up" the broader prayers and gestures that accompany the essential rite of each sacrament. Rather, the Church promulgates the fuller rites so that each sacrament is celebrated in a fashion that does justice to the spiritual profundity of what is taking place. As Aquinas explains, "Human institutions observed in the sacraments are not essential to the sacrament; but belong to the solemnity which is added to the sacraments in order to arouse devotion and reverence in the recipients."[6]

Following the seminal passage in James 5, the *Catechism* outlines the essential rite of Anointing of the Sick in this way: "The celebration of the sacrament includes the following principal elements: the 'priests of the Church'—in silence—lay hands on the sick; they pray over them in the faith of the Church—this is the epiclesis proper to this sacrament; they then anoint them with oil blessed, if possible, by the bishop."[7]

Normally the priest anoints the sick with blessed oil twice, first on the forehead and then on the hands. When anointing the forehead, the priests says: "Through this holy anointing, may the Lord in his love and mercy help you with the grace of the Holy Spirit."[8] While anointing the hands,

---

[6] Aquinas, *ST* III, q. 64, a. 2, p. 45. See also Sr. Thomas Augustine Becker, O.P., "The Role of *Solemnitas* in the Liturgy according to Saint Thomas Aquinas," in *Rediscovering Aquinas and the Sacraments*, ed. Michael Dauphinais and Matthew Levering (Chicago: Hillenbrand Books, 2009), 114–35.

[7] *CCC*, 1519.

[8] *Pastoral Care of the Sick: Rites of Anointing and Viaticum* (Collegeville, MN: The Liturgical Press, 1983), 94 [at §124].

the priest prays: "May the Lord who frees you from sin save you and raise you up."[9] These anointings signify and clarify that the ill and suffering person—precisely as being in danger of death—has been joined to and will be strengthened by God and freed from sin.

The extraordinary form of Extreme Unction includes anointings of the eyes, ears, nose, mouth, hands, and feet.[10] The words that the priest uses when making these additional anointings clarify that they are aimed at obtaining forgiveness for the sins that the recipient may have committed with these various powers: "Through this holy anointing and through His tender mercy may the Lord forgive you whatever sins you have committed through sight, . . . hearing, . . . smell, . . . taste, . . . and power of speech, . . . touch, . . . power of walking."[11]

The symbolism of the priestly anointing is a significant disclosure of the purpose of the sacrament. "When the frightening memory of past sins, heighted by the present weakness and a premonition of imminent death," O'Neill explains, "tempts the Christian to despair, the priest brings the healing oil to anoint the senses, represented by the head and

---

9   *Pastoral Care of the Sick*, 94 [at §124].

10 For a summary of the practice of Anointing of the Sick in the Orthodox Churches of the Christian East, see Levering's summary of the work of Paul Meyendorff in *Dying and the Virtues* (Grand Rapids, MI: William B. Eerdmans Publishing Company, 2018), 276, note 15.

11 From the *Roman Ritual*, §35, cited by Daniel G. Van Slyke in *Liturgy 101: Sacraments and Sacramentals* (Liguori, MO: Liguori Publications, 2010), 99.

the hands, which has so often led to sin."[12]

Because the exact moment when one might suffer a condition that places them in proximity to death cannot always be known in advance, and also because of the diversity of conditions and illnesses, the Church has promulgated a number of official rites for the celebration of Anointing of the Sick that adapt the rite to various circumstances. These diverse celebrations all contain the same essential rite for the administration of Anointing of the Sick, but they allow for some elasticity due to the unpredictability of conditions and circumstances of the recipient. There are three broad scenarios that the Church promulgates the rite of anointing for: outside of Mass, within Mass, and anointing in a hospital or institution.

A communal celebration in the context of the Eucharistic liturgy has a special significance because the recipient benefits from the prayers of the community and the reception of Holy Communion in the context of the Mass. However, this scenario presupposes that the condition of illness is known adequately in advance to allow for the required planning and that the nature of the condition makes participation in a public Mass possible and not burdensome for the patient.

There are many good (and some necessary) reasons why the celebration of the sacrament should take place outside of Mass in certain situations. In these cases, the broader rite can be adapted to the situation. Each of the variations of the rite allows

---

[12] Colman E. O'Neill, *Meeting Christ in the Sacraments* (New York: Alba House, 1991), 290.

for Penance to be celebrated and Holy Communion to be received as Viaticum along with Anointing of the Sick, if time, health condition, and the circumstances allow. If the condition and circumstances are such that only the most essential aspects of the rite can be celebrated, the Church also promulgates "rites for exceptional circumstances."[13] These rites are to be used when "sudden illness or an accident or some other cause has placed one of the faithful in the proximate or immediate danger of death."[14] The scene of an accident or other emergency scenarios are obviously the context of these rites.

Depending on the severity of the circumstance, there are two principal forms of celebration that apply to these cases. One is a "Continuous Rite of Penance, Anointing, and Viaticum," which allows for Communion to be omitted, if the recipient is not in a condition to receive.[15] The second form is a "Rite for Emergencies," which is to be used "if death seems imminent and there is not enough time to celebrate the three sacraments in the manner given in the continuous rite."[16]

As the words said by the priest for each anointing indicate ("Through this holy anointing, may the Lord in his love and mercy help you with the

---

[13] See *Pastoral Care of the Sick*, 200.

[14] *Pastoral Care of the Sick*, 200 [§232].

[15] The plenary indulgence known as the Apostolic Pardon is normally not granted when Anointing of the Sick is celebrated by itself. However, the "Continuous Rite of Penance, Anointing, and Viaticum" does include the conferral of the Apostolic Pardon either at the conclusion of the celebration of Penance or during the Penitential Rite portion of the continuous celebration.

[16] *Pastoral Care of the Sick*, 200 [§234].

grace of the Holy Spirit [and] May the Lord who frees you from sin save you and raise you up"), the gesture of anointing with oil and the corresponding words symbolize the effects of divine "help" by grace and freedom from sin unto salvation and eternal life. "How fitting," Matthew Levering observes, "it is for the priest to beg not medical doctors but God for the grace of healing—a healing that must inevitably be primarily from sin."[17]

The gesture of anointing with oil and the specification of the gesture by the words teach us that this sacrament gives the sick special help from God so that they may be gently healed from sin and brought to eternal life.[18] When Holy Communion is given as Viaticum (food for the journey) with Anointing of the Sick, after the sick person receives Communion and answers, "Amen," the priest adds, "May the Lord Jesus Christ protect you and lead you to eternal life."[19]

The sacramental rites of the Church reveal the truth of God's ongoing salvific activity in the world. The rite of Anointing of the Sick is no exception to this. "Both word and symbolic action,"

---

[17] Levering, *Dying and the Virtues* (Grand Rapids, MI: William B. Eerdmans Publishing Company, 2018), 143.

[18] In *Dying and the Virtues*, Levering summarizes Aquinas's explanation of the symbolism of the use of oil: "Aquinas explores the fittingness of the oil of anointing in light of the analogy between bodily healing and spiritual healing" (142). As he notes, "oil 'has a softening effect, it penetrates to the very heart of a thing, and spreads over it' (suppl., q. 29, a. 4). Likewise, spiritual healing 'ought also to be gentle, lest hope, of which the dying stand in utmost need, be shattered rather than fostered' (Suppl., q. 29, a. 4)" (142).

[19] *Pastoral Care of the Sick*, 224 [§267]

Colman O'Neill explains, "invite those who suffer to discover within their own present experience the existential significance of the Christian approach to sickness and death; and there is every reason to believe that Christ, to whom the sick person is commended, uses word and symbol and the experience to which they are addressed, as ways of drawing to himself those who suffer."[20]

The Minister of the Rite

Lay people and deacons are not valid ministers of the Sacrament of Anointing of the Sick. Additionally, it is important to clarify that this anointing is not for the sake of extending a charismatic gift of healing to the sick. In fact, it should be noted that nonsacramental prayers for healing, healing prayer services, and other such spiritual activities are not to be confused with the sacramental healing conferred in Anointing of the Sick. The Church recognizes that Christians have always, rightly, prayed to God for both health of mind and body. The Church also recognizes that some individuals who are not priests may have special (charismatic) gifts related to healing. However, the Church also insists that the healing available in the sacraments, especially Anointing of the Sick, must not be confused with what may be granted by God in nonsacramental forms of prayer: "Confusion between such free non-liturgical prayer meetings

---

[20] Colman E. O'Neill, O.P., *Sacramental Realism: A General Theory of the Sacraments* (Chicago: Midwest Theological Forum, 1998), 201–2.

and liturgical celebrations properly so-called is to be carefully avoided."[21] Because of some abuses and confusion on this point, the Congregation for the Doctrine of the Faith issued a *Note on the Minister of the Sacrament of Anointing of the Sick* reasserting the position of the Church that "only priests (Bishops and presbyters) are ministers of the Anointing of the Sick."[22] This teaching, the Note clarifies, "is *definitive tenenda*. Neither deacons nor lay persons may exercise the said ministry, and any action in this regard constitutes a simulation of the Sacrament."[23]

The "anointing" of this sacrament is a consecration to Christ of the sick person in their weakened condition. As such, it is a priestly or sacerdotal ministry that can only be performed by those who participate in Christ's priesthood by means of ordination. The diaconate does not transmit powers to perform formal priestly actions. Because Anointing of the Sick is a sacramental anointing deriving from Christ's own redemptive mission, which can, when needed, remit sins, it must be administered by a priest (or bishop). In an accompanying commentary on the *Note on the Minister of the Sacrament*

---

[21] Congregation for the Doctrine of the Faith, *Instruction on Prayers for Healing* (September 14, 2000), art. 5, §2, https://www.vatican.va/roman_curia/congregations/cfaith/documents/rc_con_cfaith_doc_20001123_istruzione_en.html.

[22] Congregation for the Doctrine of the Faith, *Note on the Minister of the Sacrament of Anointing of the Sick* (February 11, 2005), https://www.vatican.va/roman_curia/congregations/cfaith/documents/rc_con_cfaith_doc_20050211_unzione-infermi_en.html.

[23] Congregation for the Doctrine of the Faith, *Minister of the Sacrament of Anointing*.

of Anointing of the Sick, Cardinal Ratzinger clarifies this point:

> In the administration of the sacraments, [the priest] acts *in persona Christi Capitis* and *in persona Ecclesiae.* The person who acts in this Sacrament is Jesus Christ; the priest is the living and visible instrument. He represents and makes Christ present in a special way, which is why the Sacrament has special dignity and efficacy in comparison with a sacramental.[24]

Furthermore, among the properly *sacramental* effects bestowed by this sacrament, the forgiveness of sins and the remnants of sin are included. The power by which sin is forgiven is the power of Christ's priesthood. For all of these reasons, therefore, the Church has consistently maintained that only priests may administer the sacrament.

The matter and form of the Anointing of the Sick, the gestures, and the variations of the rite should remind us that the external aspects of the sacrament signify internal spiritual realities. Commenting on the signification of anointing the sick with oil, John Boyle observes:

> Extreme Unction is spiritual medicine, signified by medicinal bodily anointing. If it is medicine, then there must be an illness; spiritual illness is sin and its effects,

---

[24] Congregation for the Doctrine of the Faith, *Minister of the Sacrament of Anointing.*

and thus it would follow that Extreme Unction as medicine is ordered to the healing of sin. But this raises a question: How does Extreme Unction differ from Baptism and Penance, both of which also directly heal man of sin? . . . Baptism brings about new life, Penance raises from the dead, Extreme Unction heals the sick. . . . Penance is ordered to the resuscitation of the spiritually dead, while Extreme Unction is ordered to the healing of the spiritually living but sick.[25]

The study of the rites of the sacraments and the proper minister should always be informed by the theology of the sacraments. In the case of Anointing of the Sick, the anointing of those gravely ill with oil, along with the priestly prayer, mediates Christ's salvific, priestly healing to those most in need of it.

---

[25] John Boyle, "Saint Thomas Aquinas on the Anointing of the Sick," in *Rediscovering Aquinas and the Sacraments*, ed. Michael Dauphinais and Matthew Levering (Chicago: Hillenbrand Books, 2009), 78.

CHAPTER VI

THE CHRISTIAN ATTITUDE TOWARD DEATH AND BASIC BIOETHICAL PRINCIPLES

Is Death to Be Celebrated or Mourned by Christians?

So is death, ultimately, from a Christian viewpoint something bad? Yes. Death was not part of God's original plan for the human race. In Christ, however, death has been conquered and redeemed. It is not futile. Satan is no longer victorious in death. Salvation is so complete that by his resurrection Christ has conquered death. Eternal life will be bodily for all human beings, whether in heaven or hell.

What, then, is the proper Christian attitude toward death? Since Christ has conquered death, should Christians celebrate the passing of a loved one? Is boldly hastening toward death the proper response to Christ's resurrection and ascension into heaven? The proper Christian response should be clear: even though death is defeated and believers can live their lives in hope of eternal life, death is still sad and foreboding. God has redeemed mankind from eternal loss in Christ, but death entails suffering and depravations that are not desirous in themselves, even if good can be brought from them.

Christ's own life provides powerful clarification for his followers about the proper Christian attitude toward death. Despite enjoying unbreakable intimacy with the Father, Jesus did not approach his own death in a foolhardy manner. On the night before his death in the Garden of Gethsemane, Jesus tells his disciples, "My soul is very sorrowful, even to death" (Matt 26:38). He also prays, "My Father, if it be possible, let this chalice pass from me; nevertheless, not as I will, but as you will" (Matt 26:39). Furthermore, when he joins the group mourning the death of his friend Lazarus, we are told that "Jesus wept" (John 11:35).[1]

The Lord's behavior toward his own death and that of Lazarus clearly indicates that mourning is a proper Christian response to death, even though in faith we profess Christ's ultimate victory and commend the deceased to eternal life. Why, then, is mourning appropriate? The loss of a loved one or the prospect of losing one's own life is just

---

[1] For a presentation of Christian attitudes toward death and end-of-life situations, see Esther E. Acolatse, "Embracing and Resisting Death: A Theology of Justice and Hope for Care at the End of Life," in *Living Well and Dying Faithfully: Christian Practices for End-of-Life Care*, ed. John Swinton and Richard Payne (Grand Rapids, MI: William B. Eerdmans Publishing Company, 2009), especially 246–71.

that—loss. The faith teaches that the loss is not total or permanent, but it is, nevertheless, a loss. Measured sadness in the face of loss is not only reasonable, but it is also appropriate. Christ's own attitude toward the loss of his friend Lazarus and toward his approaching passion confirm this conclusion. Fr. Bryan Kromholtz insightfully explains the suitability of Christian mourning by clarifying its object:

> When we lose a loved one, our full reunion with that deceased person can take place only at the end. And of course, in the meantime, death has taken this person away from us. The person is with us no more—at least as a complete, human person. . . .
>
> Death is the loss of the body for everyone, including the holiest of saints. This may be understood as a reason that we are to mourn, and the reason that Jesus recoiled at his own death. Our words, our preaching, can allow for tears to be shed at this loss, even as it offers reason to hope that every tear will finally be wiped away.[2]

Death is a true loss and privation; we can no longer be in the presence of the deceased. Mourning is not a denial of Christ's victory or eternal life. Mourning is the appropriate response to the loss of the presence of the person who has passed from the earthly lives of those who remain. That someone lived a

---

[2] Bryan Kromholtz, O.P., "It Is Right to Mourn: Toward Funerals that Acknowledge Death as Loss and Lack," *Antiphon* 20, no. 1 (2016): 37–38.

saintly life, or at least appeared to die reconciled and in union with Christ, is a great consolation. Nevertheless, missing the deceased in this life is a genuine sadness. Parents who have lost children are not usually consoled by hearing the common refrain that they now have "an angel in heaven." It is perfectly right for those who have suffered the loss of a loved one to genuinely miss them and, therefore, mourn their passing—even while hoping that they are likely now in a "better place."

Likewise, even if those who are facing death are truly at peace and ready to meet Christ, they too have to face loss and deprivation—of their loved ones and their bodily integrity. They will be deprived of their bodily life, for a time, and rightfully may experience sorrow at the prospect of parting with their surviving loved ones. Sadness, mourning, and fear are not to be confused with each other. A measured mourning at the suffering and imperfection that we must endure as a result of sin is one of the interior beatitudes of the New Law. Christ promises that those who mourn will ultimately "be comforted" (Matt 5:4).

Cardinal Sarah gently reminds us that "sickness is intrinsically connected with eternity. The real men of God have no fear of death, because they are waiting for heaven."[3] The waiting and patience of the Christian's pilgrim journey, however, requires the support of grace. The graces of Anointing of the Sick help the dying to keep fear and sadness within the order of reason. However, being sad at

---

[3] Robert Cardinal Sarah, *The Power of Silence: Against the Dictatorship of Noise*, trans. Michael Miller (San Francisco: Ignatius Press, 2017), 179 (no. 343).

the prospect of passing ought not be confused with fear. Fear of the Lord, properly understood, has a healthy place in Christian morality and spirituality. However, just because a dying person is sad to part with their loved ones, or the loved ones mourn the death of the deceased, does not mean that they have succumbed to irrational fear.

Fr. Kromholtz has identified two common approaches to death that are often manifest in the preaching at funeral Masses or in attempts to console those suffering the loss. Both fall short of an informed Christian understanding of death. On the one hand, Christians frequently turn funerals into what Kromholtz calls a "non-eschatological" celebration of life. In these cases, "the death of the deceased person is treated primarily as an occasion for the summing up of that person's completed life, normally with a focus on its positive aspects."[4] Kromholtz describes this approach to death as "non-eschatological" because "it does not offer any hint of an expectation for the future fulfillment of promises, let alone the coming of Christ. . . . In such an approach, there can even be a lack of reference to anything spiritual or transcendent."[5] On the other hand, Kromholtz describes another response to death as a "celebration of afterlife." This attitude, he explains, "involves a focus on personal eschatology—usually with optimistic overtones. Such a way of dealing with death proclaims with assurance that the deceased is already in heaven (or even 'already raised' from the dead)."[6]

---

[4] Kromholtz, "It Is Right to Mourn," 22.
[5] Kromholtz, "It Is Right to Mourn," 22.
[6] Kromholtz, "It Is Right to Mourn," 25.

It is important—pivotal—that life be understood from a perspective of eternity. Cardinal Sarah underscores this point with the following words:

> Church teaching about death does not seek first to console or to reassure the bereaved with soothing words. Following Christ, she intends to speak about the immortality of the soul and the resurrection of the body. In Preface I for the Dead, we find this statement: "Life is changed not ended, and, when this earthly dwelling turns to dust, an eternal dwelling is made ready for them in heaven."[7]

In her prayer, the Church does not view the life of the deceased as ended, nor does she rob Christ of his role as the judge of each soul that has passed from this life by prematurely canonizing them. The Church commends the dead to God and affirms that their life has not ended but changed.

Anointing of the Sick, Care for the Dying, and the Value of Suffering: Some (Very) Basic Bioethical Guidance

By joining the sick person to Christ and strengthening them against temptation, the Sacrament of Anointing of the Sick makes illness and dying a great source of spiritual fruitfulness. As we saw

---

[7] Sarah, *The Power of Silence*, 183–84 (no. 356).

above, the post-Christian world rejects the idea that life and death have a meaning and purpose, and therefore this world seeks to avoid death and deny suffering at all costs. Interventions into end-of-life situations like euthanasia and physician-assisted suicide have as their basis and motivating principle the belief that suffering is intolerable, baseless, and pointless. Anointing of the Sick helps to clarify the Christian response to the problem of suffering and evil.[8]

Euthanasia and physician-assisted suicide are actions that bring about the death of the sick, vulnerable, and dying for the sake of eliminating their suffering.[9] The Christian tradition teaches that any direct action or omission aimed at ending a human life is a violation of the Fifth Commandment: thou shalt not kill. The Church's teaching on this matter is extremely clear: "An act or omission which, of itself or by intention, causes death in order to eliminate suffering constitutes a murder gravely contrary to the dignity of the human person and to the respect due to the living God, his

---

[8] For recent magisterial guidance for pastors on the administration of Penance, Anointing of the Sick, and Viaticum in the current context in which actions like euthanasia may be encouraged by health care institutions, see the Congregation for the Doctrine of the Faith's Letter "Samaritanus Bonus: On the Care of Persons in the Critical and Terminal Phases of Life" (July 14, 2020), §10–11, http://www.vatican.va/roman_curia/congregations/cfaith/documents/rc_con_cfaith_doc_20200714_samaritanus-bonus_en.html.

[9] For a reflection on how to integrate end-of-life bioethical issues with the Sacrament of Anointing of the Sick, see Joseph Tham, L.C., "Bioethics and Anointing of the Sick," *Studia Bioethica* 8, no. 3 (2015): 70–73.

Creator."[10] Withholding basic forms of sustenance, like hydration, to those in end-of-life situations is also to intend to end their lives. Even a perfectly healthy person in the full vigor of young adulthood would die in a matter of days without hydration. In cases of euthanasia and physician-assisted suicide, it is the act, like administering a lethal dose of a chemical or gas to bring about death, or the omission, like withholding hydration, that brings about the death of the patient, and not the illness or advanced age. Taking an action that brings about someone's death, even if they are ill or near death, is to take their lives.

This does not mean that we have to dominate the last days of someone's life with highly invasive technologies and costly medical procedures. It may be quite licit to discontinue medical procedures or further interventions when it becomes clear that death is imminent or that such procedures do not benefit the patient.[11] Accepting death and causing it are two different moral actions. The Church offers wise and balanced guidance for this situation:

> Discontinuing medical procedures that are burdensome, dangerous, extraordinary, or disproportionate to the expected out-

---

[10] *CCC*, 2277.

[11] The US Conference of Catholic Bishops has published a helpful resource authored by moral theologian Richard Doerflinger to assist families and health care workers who may be facing this dilemma: Richard Doerflinger, "Respecting the Dignity of the Human Person at the End of Life" (2015), https://www.usccb.org/beliefs-and-teachings/how-we-teach/catechesis/catechetical-sunday/human-dignity/family-resource-doerflinger.

come can be legitimate; it is the refusal of "over-zealous" treatment.

Here one does not will to cause death; one's inability to impede it is merely accepted. The decisions should be made by the patient if he is competent and able or, if not, by those legally entitled to act for the patient, whose reasonable will and legitimate interests must always be respected.[12]

Related to the error of justifying euthanasia as a means of eliminating suffering is the failure to recognize that, in light of Christ, suffering and illness are not void of meaning and purpose in God's plan of redemption. Indeed, to the contrary, Christ's own life and death clearly indicate that when embraced with the proper outlook, and in union with Christ, suffering and death are pregnant opportunities for growth toward deeper union with God and for obtaining graces for others.[13]

---

[12] *CCC*, 2278. Emphasis added.

[13] For a helpful articulation on how Catholic health care workers can integrate Anointing of the Sick with the religious assistance that their Catholic patients may need or request, see Pontifical Council for Pastoral Assistance to Health Care Workers, *New Charter for Health Care Workers* (Philadelphia: The National Catholic Bioethics Center, 2017), especially §135–39.

CONCLUSION

Returning to the overarching theme of this book, the importance of Anointing of the Sick is generally underappreciated by the faithful, and its true meaning is misunderstood. Looking at the meaning of the sacrament from what is indicated by the rite itself, it is easy to see that what the faithful ought to expect from this sacrament is not, in the first place, a miraculous cure from their ailment. "All of this is ordered to this end," John Boyle explains, "that nothing should remain in man that might impede the soul in coming to perceive the glory of God upon leaving the body."[1] By the hidden help of the graces within the soul that it causes, Anointing of the Sick draws the recipients closer to Christ, strengthens them against sin and temptation amidst the difficulty and trauma of facing death, consecrates suffering and death to God through Christ, and carries them from earthly to eternal life. Heaven is the true home of the faithful. Christ's kingdom is not "of this world" (John 18:36).

---

[1] John Boyle, "Saint Thomas Aquinas on the Anointing of the Sick," in *Rediscovering Aquinas and the Sacraments*, ed. Michael Dauphinais and Matthew Levering (Chicago: Hillenbrand Books, 2009), 81.

As a result, Anointing of the Sick both signifies and causes the recipient's final reconciliation
with God in Christ. Deepening in the sick person
the saving work begun in Baptism, this last sacrament accomplishes ultimate reconciliation between
the sinner and God, as John Paul II explains: "The
anointing of the sick in the trial of illness and old
age and especially at the Christian's final hour is a
sign of definitive conversion to the Lord and of total
acceptance of suffering and death as a penance for
sins. And in this is accomplished supreme reconciliation with the Father."[2] What a gift!

Christianity is not just a hypothetical answer
to the problem of death and the question of what
happens after death; rather, the Christian faith is
rooted in Christ's actual victory over death. The
great Father of the Church St. Athanasius observes
that "for men who, before they believe in Christ,
think death horrible and are afraid of it, once
they are converted despise it so completely that
they go eagerly to meet it, and themselves become
witnesses of the Saviour's resurrection from it."[3]
The risen Christ changes completely how people
ought to view death. No longer is death a last
word, let alone a total loss. The death of the follower of Christ, Bernard of Clairvaux preaches,
"is good, because it ends his miseries; it is better
still, because he begins a new life; it is excellent,

---

[2] St. John Paul II, *Reconciliation and Penance* (December 2,
1984), §27, http://www.vatican.va/content/john-paul-ii/en/
apost_exhortations/documents/hf_jp-ii_exh_02121984_rec-
onciliatio-et-paenitentia.html.

[3] St. Athanasius, *On the Incarnation* (New York: St. Vladimir's
Seminary Press, 1998), 57.

because it places him in sweet security. From his bed of mourning . . . Jesus acknowledges him as his brother and friend, for he has died to the world before closing his eyes from its dazzling light. Such is the death of the saints, a death very precious in the sight of God."[4]

The creation story narrated in the first chapter of the Bible culminates in the day of the Lord's rest—the Sabbath. For this reason, the Christian faith teaches that human existence is not defined by the toil and labor of the fallen world. Christ's resurrection fulfills and completes the Sabbath rest. Each week the Church gathers to commemorate Christ's victory over death in the Sunday celebration of the Eucharist. John Paul II ties these points together:

> Christ's Resurrection and the weekly recurrence of this solemn memorial help to remind us of *the pilgrim and eschatological character of the People of God.* Sunday after Sunday the Church moves towards the final "Lord's Day," that Sunday which knows no end. The expectation of Christ's coming is inscribed in the very mystery of the Church and is evidenced in every Eucharistic celebration. But, with its specific remembrance of the glory of the Risen Christ, the Lord's Day recalls with greater

---

4 St. Bernard of Clairvaux, quoted in Charles Kenny, *Half Hours with the Saints and Servants of God* (London: Burns and Oates, 1882), 450, cited in Scott Hahn, *Hope to Die: The Christian Meaning of Death and the Resurrection of the Body* (Steubenville, OH: Emmaus Road Publishing, 2020), 115.

intensity the future glory of his "return." This makes Sunday the day on which the Church, showing forth more clearly her identity as "Bride," anticipates in some sense the eschatological reality of the heavenly Jerusalem. Gathering her children into the Eucharistic assembly and teaching them to wait for the "divine Bridegroom," she engages in a kind of "exercise of desire," receiving a foretaste of the joy of the new heavens and new earth, when the holy city, the new Jerusalem, will come down from God, "prepared as a bride adorned for her husband" (Rev 21:2).[5]

Just as the Christian people enter each week into the rest of the Lord's Day, so too is the death of every soul claimed by Christ a final Passover into the eternal Sabbath of the risen Lord. Each and every human life is a gift from God. Our lives and our deaths are not our own. St. Paul reminds the Christians in Rome that "None of us lives to himself, and none of us dies to himself. If we live, we live to the Lord, and if we die, we die to the Lord; so then, whether we live or whether we die, we are the Lord's" (Rom 14:7–8). To be guided by the reign of the risen Lord, to truly live the dogma of Christ, the Christian faithful have to live *and* die for Christ. By turning to the helping and healing graces of Anointing of the Sick, the faithful end their earthly lives living the truth of Christ, which

---

[5]   St. John Paul II, *Dies Domini* (May 31, 1998), §37, http://www.vatican.va/content/john-paul-ii/en/apost_letters/1998/documents/hf_jp-ii_apl_05071998_dies-domini.html.

carries them unto the rest of eternal glory. "To die is gain."

Bibliography

Acolatse, Esther E. "Embracing and Resisting Death: A Theology of Justice and Hope for Care at the End of Life." In *Living Well and Dying Faithfully: Christian Practices for End-of-Life Care*. Edited by John Swinton and Richard Payne. Grand Rapids, MI: William B. Eerdmans Publishing Company, 2009.

Aquinas, Thomas. *Commentary on the Sentences*. Vol. 8, book IV, distinctions 14–25. Translated by Beth Mortensen. Green Bay, WI: Aquinas Institute, Inc., 2017.

———. *Summa contra gentiles*. Book 4, *Salvation*. Translated by Charles O'Neil. Notre Dame, IN: University of Notre Dame Press, 1957.

———. *Summa theologiae*. Vol. 13. Edited by John Mortensen and Enrique Alarcon. Translated by Laurence Shapcote, O.P. Lander, WY: The Aquinas Institute for the Study of Sacred Doctrine, 2012.

———. *Summa theologiae*. Vol. 16. Edited by John Mortensen and Enrique Alarcon. Translated by Laurence Shapcote, O.P. Lander, WY: The Aquinas Institute for the Study of Sacred Doctrine, 2012.

———. *Summa theologiae*. Vol. 18. Edited by John Mortensen and Enrique Alarcon. Translated by Laurence Shapcote, O.P. Lander, WY: The Aquinas Institute for the Study of Sacred Doctrine, 2012.

———. *Summa theologiae*. Vol. 20. Edited by John Mortensen and Enrique Alarcon. Translated by Laurence Shapcote, O.P. Lander, WY: The Aquinas Institute for the Study of Sacred Doctrine, 2012.

Aristotle's De Anima in the Version of William Moerbeke and the Commentary of St. Thomas Aquinas. Translated by Kenelm Foster and Silvester Humphries. New Haven, CT: Yale University Press, 1951.

Athanasius, St. *On the Incarnation*. New York: St. Vladimir's Seminary Press, 1998.

Becker, O.P., Sr. Thomas Augustine. "The Role of *Solemnitas* in the Liturgy according to Saint Thomas Aquinas." In *Rediscovering Aquinas and the Sacraments*. Edited by Michael Dauphinais and Matthew Levering. Chicago: Hillenbrand Books, 2009.

Bellarmine, St. Robert. *The Art of Dying Well (or, How to Be a Saint, Now and Forever)*. Manchester: Sophia Institute Press, 2005.

Boyle, John. "Saint Thomas Aquinas on the Anointing of the Sick." In *Rediscovering Aquinas and the Sacraments*. Edited by Michael Dauphinais and Matthew Levering. Chicago: Hillenbrand Books, 2009.

Calvin, John. *Institutes of the Christian Religion*. Vol. 2. Translated by Henry Beveridge. London: James Clarke and Co., 1962.

Camus, Albert. *The Myth of Sisyphus and Other Essays*. Translated by Justin O'Brien. New

York: Vintage Books, 1991.

Catechism of the Catholic Church, 2nd ed. New York: Doubleday, 1995.

Cessario, O.P., Romanus. "Anointing of the Sick: The Sanctification of Human Suffering." *Nova et Vetera* 17, no. 2 (2019): 297–307.

———. *The Godly Image: Christian Satisfaction in Aquinas*. Washington, D.C.: The Catholic University of America Press, 2020.

Choron, Jacques. *Death and Western Thought*. New York: Macmillan, 1963.

The Code of Canon Law. The Holy See. 1983. vatican.va/archive/cod-iuris-canonici/cic_index_en.html.

Congregation for the Doctrine of the Faith. *Instruction on Prayers for Healing*. The Holy See. September 14, 2000. https://www.vatican.va/roman_curia/congregations/cfaith/documents/rc_con_cfaith_doc_20001123_istruzione_en.html.

———. *Note on the Minister of the Sacrament of Anointing of the Sick*. The Holy See. February 11, 2005. https://www.vatican.va/roman_curia/congregations/cfaith/documents/rc_con_cfaith_doc_20050211_unzione-infermi_en.html.

———. Letter "Samaritanus Bonus: On the Care of Persons in the Critical and Terminal Phases of Life." The Holy See. July 14, 2020. http://www.vatican.va/roman_curia/congregations/cfaith/documents/rc_con_cfaith_doc_20200714_samaritanus-bonus_en.html.

Connors, Ryan. "Holy Anointing Makes Holy Suffering." Unpublished paper.

Council of Trent, in *Decrees of the Ecumenical Councils*. Vol. 2, *Trent to Vatican II*. Edited by Norman P. Tanner, S.J. Washington, D.C.: Georgetown University Press, 1990.

Denzinger, Henrich. *Compendium of Creeds, Definitions, and Declarations on Matters of Faith and Morals*. 43rd ed. Edited by Peter Hünermann. San Francisco: Ignatius Press, 2012.

DiNoia, O.P., J. Augustine, and Joseph Fox, O.P. "Priestly Dimensions of the Sacrament of the Anointing of the Sick," *The Priest* 62 (2006): 10–13.

Doerflinger, Richard. "Respecting the Dignity of the Human Person at the End of Life." Usccb.org. 2015. https://www.usccb.org/beliefs-and-teachings/how-we-teach/catechesis/catechetical-sunday/human-dignity/family-resource-doerflinger.

Dugdale, L. S. *The Lost Art of Dying: Reviving Forgotten Wisdom*. New York: Harper Collins Publishers, 2020.

Emery, O.P., Giles. "Reconciliation with the Church and Interior Penance: The Contribution of Thomas Aquinas on the Question of the *Res et Sacramentum* of Penance." *Nova et Vetera* 1, no. 2 (2003): 283–302.

Fastiggi, Robert. *The Sacrament of Reconciliation: An Anthropological and Scriptural Understanding*. Chicago/Mundelein: Hillenbrand Books, 2017.

Francis, Pope. *Laudato Si'*. The Holy See. May 24, 2015. https://www.vatican.va/content/francesco/en/encyclicals/documents/papa-francesco_20150524_enciclica-laudato-si.html.

Gerosa, Libero. *Canon Law*. New York: Continuum, 2002.

Gregory of Nyssa. *The Life of Moses*. Translated by Abraham J. Malherbe. San Francisco: Harper San Francisco, 2006.

Guerra, Marc D. "The Use and Abuse of Thanatos in Life." *Perspectives on Political Science* 37, no. 3 (2008): 136–41.

Hahn, Scott. *Hope to Die*: *The Christian Meaning of Death and the Resurrection of the Body*. Steubenville, OH: Emmaus Road Publishing, 2020.

Healy, Mary. *The Gospel of Mark*. Catholic Commentary on Sacred Scripture. Grand Rapids, MI: Baker Academic, 2008.

Huxley, Aldous. *Brave New World*. New York: Harper and Row, 1989.

Ignatius of Antioch, St. "The Epistle of Ignatius to the Romans." Translated by Alexander Roberts and James Donaldson. In vol. 1 of *Ante-Nicene Fathers*. Edited by Alexander Roberts, James Donaldson, and A. Cleveland Coxe. Buffalo, NY: Christian Literature Publishing Co., 1885. https://www.newadvent.org/fathers/0107.htm.

John Paul II, St. *Dies Domini*. The Holy See. May 31, 1998. http://www.vatican.va/content/john-paul-ii/en/apost_letters/1998/documents/hf_jp-ii_apl_05071998_dies-domini.html.

———. *Dominum et Vivificantem: On the Holy Spirit in the Life of the Church and the World*. The Holy See. May 18, 1986. http://www.vatican.va/content/john-paul-ii/en/encyclicals/

documents/hf_jp-ii_enc_18051986_dominum-et-vivificantem.html.

———. *Evangelium Vitae*. The Holy See. March 25, 1995. http://www.vatican.va/content/john-paul-ii/en/encyclicals/documents/hf_jp-ii_enc_25031995_evangelium-vitae.html.

———. *Letter of His Holiness Pope John Paul II to the Elderly*. The Holy See. 1999. http://www.vatican.va/content/john-paul-ii/en/letters/1999/documents/hf_jp-ii_let_01101999_elderly.html.

———. *Reconciliation and Penance*. The Holy See. December 2, 1984. http://www.vatican.va/content/john-paul-ii/en/apost_exhortations/documents/hf_jp-ii_exh_02121984_reconciliatio-et-paenitentia.html.

———. *Redemptoris Mater: On the Blessed Virgin Mary in the Life of the Pilgrim Church*. The Holy See. March 25, 1987. http://www.vatican.va/content/john-paul-ii/en/encyclicals/documents/hf_jp-ii_enc_25031987_redemptoris-mater.html.

———. *Salvifici Doloris*. The Holy See. February 11, 1984. http://www.vatican.va/content/john-paul-ii/en/apost_letters/1984/documents/hf_jp-ii_apl_11021984_salvifici-doloris.html.

Journet, Charles. *The Meaning of Grace*. Translated by A. V. Littledale. Princeton: Scepter Publishers, 1996.

Kasza, John C. *Understanding Sacramental Healing: Anointing and Viaticum*. Chicago: Hillenbrand Books, 2007.

———. "Anointing of the Sick." In *The Oxford

Handbook of Sacramental Theology. Edited by Hans Boersma and Matthew Levering, 558–71. Oxford: Oxford University Press, 2015.

Keller, O.P., Paul Jerome. *101 Questions & Answers on the Sacraments of Healing*: *Penance and Anointing of the Sick*. New York/Mahwah: Paulist Press, 2010.

Kenny, Charles. *Half Hours with the Saints and Servants of God*. London: Burns and Oates, 1882.

Kromholtz, O.P., Bryan. "It Is Right to Mourn: Toward Funerals that Acknowledge Death as Loss and Lack." *Antiphon* 20, no. 1 (2016): 37–38.

Meyendorff, Paul. *The Anointing of the Sick*. Crestwood, NY: St. Vladimir's Seminary Press, 2009.

Larson-Miller, Lizette. *The Sacrament of Anointing of the Sick*. Collegeville, MN: Liturgical Press, 2005.

Leget, Carlo. *Living with God: Thomas Aquinas on the Relation between Life on Earth and "Life" after Death*. Leuven: Peeters, 1997.

Levering, Matthew. *Dying and the Virtues*. Grand Rapids, MI: William B. Eerdmans Publishing Company, 2018.

———. Introduction to *On Christian Dying*. Edited by Matthew Levering. Lanham: Rowman and Littlefield Publishers, Inc., 2004.

———. *Jesus and the Demise of Death*: *Resurrection, Afterlife, and the Fate of the Christian*. Waco, TX: Baylor University Press, 2012.

Luther, Martin. *Pagan Servitude of the Church* (Babylonian Captivity). In *Martin Luther*.

Edited by John Dillenberger. New York: Anchor Books, 1961.

Muggeridge, Malcolm. *Something Beautiful for God: Mother Teresa of Calcutta*. San Francisco: Harper and Row, 1971.

Nietzsche, Friedrich. *Thus Spoke Zarathustra*. In *The Portable Nietzsche*. Translated by Walter Kaufmann. New York: The Viking Press, 1964.

Nutt, Roger W. *General Principles of Sacramental Theology*. Washington D.C.: The Catholic University of America Press, 2017.

———. "'Obedient unto Death': The Function of Philippians 2 in St. Thomas's Theology of the Cross." In *Thomas Aquinas, Biblical Theologian*. Edited by Michael Dauphinais and Roger Nutt. Steubenville, OH: Emmaus Academic, 2021, 231–47.

O'Neill, O.P., Colman E. *Meeting Christ in the Sacraments*. New York: Alba House, 1991.

———. *Sacramental Realism*: *A General Theory of the Sacraments*. Chicago: Midwest Theological Forum, 1998.

Pastoral Care of the Sick: Rites of Anointing and Viaticum. Collegeville, MN: The Liturgical Press, 1983.

Paul VI, Pope. *Sacram Unctione Infirmorum: On the Sacrament of Anointing of the Sick*. The Holy See. November 13, 1972. http://www.vatican.va/content/paul-vi/en/apost_constitutions/documents/hf_p-vi_apc_19721130_sacram-unctionem.html.

Plato. *Apology*. Translated by Benjamin Jowett. Accessed on November 11, 2020. http://classics.mit.edu/Plato/apology.html.

Ponticus, Evagrius. *The Praktikos and Chapters on Prayer*. Translated by John Eudes Bamberger. Kalamazoo, MI: Cistercian Publications, 1981.

Pontifical Council for Pastoral Assistance to Health Care Workers. *New Charter for Health Care Workers*. Philadelphia: The National Catholic Bioethics Center, 2017.

Poschmann, Bernhard. *Penance and Anointing of the Sick*. Translated by Francis Courtney. New York: Herder and Herder, 1964.

Ratzinger, Joseph. *Eschatology: Death and Eternal Life*. Translated by Michael Waldstein. Washington, D.C.: The Catholic University of America Press, 1988.

Revel, Jean-Philippe. *Traité des sacrements*. Vol. 6, *L'onction des maladies: Rédemption de la chair par la chair*. Paris: Éditions du Cerf, 2009.

Sarah, Robert Cardinal. *The Power of Silence: Against the Dictatorship of Noise*. Translated by Michael Miller. San Francisco: Ignatius Press, 2017.

Sartre, Jean-Paul. *L'être and le néant* [*Being and Nothingness*]. Paris: Gallimard, 1955.

The Sayings of the Desert Fathers. Translated by Benedicta Ward, S.L.G. Trappist, KY: Cistercian Publications, 1984.

Schmemann, Alexander. *Great Lent: Journey to Pascha*. Revised and edited. Crestwood, N.Y.: St. Vladimir's Seminary Press, 1974.

Spezzano, Daria. *The Glory of God's Grace: Deification according to St. Thomas Aquinas*. Ave Maria, FL: Sapientia Press of Ave Maria

University, 2015.

Tham, L.C., Joseph. "Bioethics and Anointing of the Sick." *Studia Bioethica* 8, no. 3 (2015): 70–73.

Tolstoy, Leo. *The Death of Ivan Ilyich.* Translated by Lynn Solotaroff. New York: Bantam Books, 1981.

Van Slyke, Daniel G. *Liturgy 101: Sacraments and Sacramentals.* Liguori, MO: Liguori Publications, 2010.

Vatican Council II. *Gaudium et Spes.* The Holy See. December 7, 1965. http://www.vatican.va/archive/hist_councils/ii_vatican_council/documents/vat-ii_const_19651207_gaudium-et-spes_en.html.

———. *Lumen Gentium.* The Holy See. November 21, 1964. http://www.vatican.va/archive/hist_councils/ii_vatican_council/documents/vat-ii_const_19641121_lumen-gentium_en.html.

———. *Sacrosanctum Concilium.* In *Decrees of the Ecumenical Councils.* Vol. 2, *Trent to Vatican II.* Edited by Norman P. Tanner, S.J. Washington, D.C.: Georgetown University Press, 1990.

Index

A

abortion, 22

absolution, 40, 91–92, 135n27

action, 61, 67, 76, 80, 109, 139, 144–145, 151, 153, 163–164, 163n8; external, 30, 45; moral, 6, 164; sacred, 61, 145; sinful, 77

Adam, 31, 63–64, 66, 68–70, 73–74, 78, 81–84

afterlife, 13, 16, 129n18, 161

age of reason, 98–99

analogy, 19, 103–104, 117, 151n18; analogical, 28; analogously, 73

angel, 31, 40–41, 49, 73, 160; angelic, 28

anger, 68, 71, 78, 110

animal, 28, 30, 34, 116; -like, 17

Anointing of the Sick, 1–4, 11–12, 24, 38–42, 42n34, 45, 48, 55–56, 59, 61, 61–62n16, 63, 73, 76, 78–80, 85–89, 89n8, 91–94, 93n13, 96, 98–101, 103–104, 107, 110–111, 113–115, 118–120, 118n4, 122–123, 125–126, 125n14, 130–136, 139–140, 144–147, 148n10, 149–155, 150n15, 160, 162–163, 163n8–9, 165n13, 167–168, 170; Extreme Unction, 55, 87–88, 89n8, 117, 148, 154–155; final anointing, 87, 89, 89n8, 131; sacrament of the sick, 2–3, 5, 38, 48, 60, 88, 93

C

J

L

M

P

SCRIPTURE
REFERENCE INDEX